AMERICAN
INDIAN
WOMEN

AMERICAN INDIAN WOMEN

BY

MARION E. GRIDLEY

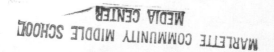
HAWTHORN BOOKS, INC.
PUBLISHERS / New York

AMERICAN INDIAN WOMEN

Library of Congress Catalog Card Number: 73-362
ISBN: 0-8015-0234-9

First Printing, February 1974
Second Printing, September 1974
Third Printing, June 1975
Fourth Printing, October 1975

CONTENTS

vi   *Contents*

AMERICAN
INDIAN
WOMEN

THE INDIAN WOMAN

When more than three hundred years pass, history often becomes blurred as legends and facts become confused. Our history books are riddled with such instances, especially with regard to the American Indian there are many misstatements arising from a basic misunderstanding of Indian people and their customs. Errors appeared in the writings of early settlers, explorers, and historians and were due mainly to this lack of understanding.

Indians and whites were miles apart in their viewpoints and their cultural concepts. Judgments were based on Anglo-Saxon and European attitudes, customs, and standards, not on Indian ones.

One of the greatest misconceptions had to do with Indian women. They were thought to have a lowly position in life, to be little respected by the men. That they were treated as slaves has been written over and over. Yet nothing was further from the truth among most tribes.

In some tribes, Indian women had considerable power, and in a number of groups they were supreme. In many cases they had a higher position in their society than

3

did women in other societies and voted long before any other women of the world did so. They could be the equals of men as warriors, and many Indian women were as famous in war as they were strong in council. Even if they did not take part in the council deliberations and decisions of the chiefs, they could still express their opinions.

In most tribes, there was a clan system. The clans were formed of related families, and marriage within a clan was therefore not permitted. The clans were usually named for birds or animals, which were thought to be the ancestors of the clan members. Each clan had a specific duty in the social structure of the tribe and in its ceremonies. Children belonged to their mothers' clan, as a rule, so the line of descent was traced through the mother. A newly married man moved into his wife's home, and left the home if the marriage broke up. If the wife wished him to leave, she had only to place his belongings outside the door of the house.

The clan system, among the Pueblos, was sharply defined and complex. The fields were owned by the various clans and were subdivided into individual family property belonging to the women. The head of the clan was the clan mother. Through her, the chiefs inherited their offices and the right to ceremonial properties and rituals.

Women were cared for and protected by the men, but they were the property owners. Not only did they own the fields, but the crops, the flocks, and the herds. They owned all household goods and the house itself.

Women could be guides, interpreters, and scouts— even negotiators for peace. They could be medicine women and chiefs. There are numbers of such women throughout Indian history.

There were powerful female spiritual forces who had much to do with the creation of the world and who were venerated in tribal religious teachings. In the South-west, among the Navajos, Changing Woman was one of these great beings.

The Navajos believed there were many Holy People, or spirit beings, and Changing Woman was the most sacred of them all. She helped to create the people of the earth, who were the ancestors of the Navajos. This was after the Holy Ones came into the world from where they lived below the surface of the earth. They made all the things of the earth, and Changing Woman taught the people how to live in harmony with all of these things— the elements, the mountains, the plants, the animals.

Not all of the Holy Ones were friendly spirits, and some of them were harmful. But Changing Woman was always kind and friendly. She had two sons called the Hero Twins, who were great warriors. Her husband was the sun. The story of the creation and of Changing Woman's part in it is kept alive in a beautiful, centuries-old religious ceremony called the Blessing Way.

Among eastern tribes there was a spirit being similar to Changing Woman, though not as powerful. This was Woman of the Sky, and she, also, had two sons. According to most accounts, one was good and the other evil. Sky Woman created the earth and her sons brought to it both good and evil things, and people became both good and evil.

In the Iroquois tribes, the confederacy of Five Nations that spread across what is now the state of New York, women had an extremely important role.

The Iroquois were governed by a council of fifty chiefs, or sachems. There was also a lesser council of "pine tree chiefs," who spoke for the people. They could not vote, but they were in a sense, "professional orators," trained in the art of public speaking from childhood.

The sachems acted for the good of the people. They were civil chiefs and while they could declare war, they could not take part in any fighting while they were in office. In their council meetings, the sachems wore deer antlers on their heads. These sachems were chosen by the women, who could also have them voted out of office, or "have the horns taken away." Although the Council of Women did not actually vote, when they announced whom they wanted as sachems, the men had to elect them.

The sachems decided and settled all matters placed before them, but to make their decisions valid, they all had to be of one mind. Nothing could be done if a vote was not unanimous. Even though they made laws, the women could overrule them if the laws were not to their liking, and the women could even order the death of a sachem.

The Iroquois made great use of wampum beads in their ceremonies. These beads were cut and hand drilled from clam shells in colors of purple, white, or a mixture of both. Strings of wampum were used to record names, and these strings were kept by the oldest woman in the clan.

When a sachem was elected to office, he was given a name and this name was "strung" in wampum. A certain arrangement of the colors would indicate the name. The wampum string was placed about the chief's neck and to "place a necklace around one's neck," was the phrase used to mean giving a name. When the chief died, the wampum string was returned to the clan mother who was the holder of the beads and the one who officiated at the name-giving ceremony.

Wampum beads were also woven into belts which were exchanged to consummate a treaty or bind an agreement. As the belt was exchanged, the chief would say, "This belt preserves my words."

The Iroquois confederacy, or the League of Five Nations, was one of the most remarkable governing structures ever formed. Parts of the constitution of the United States were based upon it.

A woman had much to do with the founding of the league, which the Indians called the Long House. The actual founder was Dekanawida, a Huron, who dreamed of a plan to restore peace among the tribes who were fighting each other almost to the death.

Dekanawida enlisted the help of Hiawatha, an Onondaga, and of Jikonsaseh, a Seneca. The two disciples traveled hundreds of miles in the effort to weld the tribes together in Dekanawida's plan for peace. Jikonsaseh was known as the Peace Queen. Sometimes she is called the "Mother of Nations."

When the Peace Queen died, she was buried in a secret grave in the land of the Senecas, one of the original Five Nations. From then on, a symbolic Peace Queen was chosen from among the direct descendants of Jikonsaseh. The last of these was Caroline Parker. She was a sister of Gen. Ely S. Parker, a brigadier-general and aide to Gen. Ulysses S. Grant during the Civil War. It was Parker who wrote up the terms of Lee's surrender, and who suggested that the Southerners be allowed to keep their horses and take them home to work their farms. After the war, Grant, then president of the United States, appointed Ely Parker commissioner of the Bureau of Indian Affairs. He was the first Indian to hold this position.

American Indians did not have any understanding of royalty or titles such as king, queen, prince, or princess before the colonists arrived in America. The Natchez of Mississippi came the closest to having a king in the sense of a ruler. He was called the Great Sun and he was carried about on a litter by his "subjects." The tribes of the Northwest coast, too, had noble families. Generally, the chiefs did not actually rule. They could not sell land because Indians did not believe in land ownership, nor could they tell their people what they must do. Decisions were made in a council meeting over which the chief presided, but they were not his individual decisions. Once a decision was made, he would have the responsibility to uphold it, provided it was agreed upon by the people. He would have the authority, too, to designate the time for the hunt, the rules of the hunt, or other matters of that nature that were not commitments of a tribal nature.

The head chiefs were not primarily warriors, but they had to prove themselves in war in order to become chiefs. The chieftainship was usually not hereditary. A war chief led in the fighting and directed the battle movements, but he did not have the power to govern or declare war.

In many tribes, each town had its own village chief who owed allegiance to the chief of the tribe, but who could also act independently.

The chief served his people and watched out for their welfare. He shared his possessions with them, and very often was the poorest man in the group. The greatest men were those who could share, not those who could store up wealth, which was not considered a virtue.

The first colonists, equating the chiefs with their kings, were the ones who bestowed royal titles on the Indians. That is why you will find many references to kings and queens and princesses among the eastern tribes who were the first to come in contact with the whites. To this day, Indian people from these tribes make use of royal titles, especially that of princess.

It was the colonists' concepts of royalty that brought about many of the early problems over land. Frequently land was "bought" with goods which to the settlers was a purchase price. To the Indians, this was a customary exchange of gifts only. The newcomers from England and Europe never really understood the Indian love of the land or their belief that it was the gift of the Great Spirit, never to be owned or sold, or that the chiefs did not have the "divine right of kings" and could not sell the land or dispose of it without the consent of their people.

Among the Cherokee, there was a women's council, as there was among the Iroquois, which could override the authority of the chiefs. Other seaboard tribes probably had similar councils. The Cherokee council was made up of one woman from each clan, chosen by the clan members. The head of this assembly was called the Beloved Woman and she spoke for the women at all meetings of the chiefs. It was said that she represented and spoke for the Great Spirit.

The Beloved Woman could determine the fate of any prisoners—whether they should live or die, whether they should go free, be held in slavery, or be adopted by the tribe. This was the only title ever given to a woman in the Cherokee tribe, and the holder of it was greatly revered.

Within Indian tribes, the duties of the man and the woman were divided. The man was the hunter and the protector of the village. He would be away on the war-path, or on hunting or trading trips, often for long periods of time. These duties meant traveling hundreds of miles, mostly on foot, over rough and rugged wilderness country. His life was constantly in danger.

When he was home, he had to work at keeping himself physically fit through hard, physical activity and athletic games. He had to make his own weapons for war and for fishing and hunting. He had to build his own traps and his own canoe or dugout. He had to make all of his tools. He had to defend his village from attack or go on raiding parties to other villages. If he were a Plains Indian, he would raid to steal horses. If he lived on the Northwest coast, he would raid for slaves. He had little or no time for idleness.

Because the woman was the creator of life, she was

concerned with anything that was directly or indirectly related to creativity. It was she who hoed the fields and planted the seeds and tended the growing crops, harvesting them when ready. Indian gardening was not overly hard work, however, because of the method of planting.

The soil was rounded up into a small hill and in the hill a dead fish was placed to enrich the soil. Corn was planted in the hill and beans and pumpkins on the hillsides. The beans would twine up the corn stalks, and the pumpkin vines would twine around the hill. In between the hills, sunflowers were planted, for the seeds were rich in oil. Only the hills needed to be weeded.

The women worked in the fields together and many hands made light work. The children helped, too. The littlest ones scared away the crows while the older children planted, weeded, and harvested alongside their mothers. The men often helped with the harvesting, with the work of tapping maple sugar trees, and with the winnowing of wild rice.

The Indians made use of many wild plants, both for food and for medicine, which the women gathered in season.

The men were the canoe and boat builders, and the builders of the various types of dwellings. Only among the southwestern Indians was this situation reversed. There, the women built the adobe houses, and the men tended the fields, which were often quite some distance away from the village. Among the Pueblos, the men were the weavers, also, although in all other tribes, weaving was the women's duty.

Women tanned the skins used for clothing. They wove the mats used for floor and house coverings. They wove baskets, made pottery or utensils of bark, did all the sewing of skin or cloth garments, and dyed the materials used for weaving or embroidery. They dried all of the foods to be stored for winter use. They cared for the children.

When the tribe was on the move, it was the women who took care of the loading and unloading of household goods. The women of the Plains also took down and put up the conical tipi house.

When you compare the domestic tasks and responsibilities of Indian women with those of pioneer women, there is no great difference. It is only in recent times that we have had the benefits of electric appliances, washers, stoves, refrigerators, and the other conveniences that have made the life of women easier as far as physical effort goes.

Indian women did not consider their lot in life a hard one. They did what had to be done for survival. They loved their children and were kind to them. Everyone, from the oldest to the youngest in the camp circle, was given some task to do. So all were secure in the thought that they were needed and wanted.

The women had their enjoyments, too. There were social events which were theirs alone—a sewing bee, for example, when new clothes or moccasins were made, or a new cover for a tipi house. They would sit and chat together while making baskets or pottery. They would go on food-gathering parties when the nuts were ready, or the berries ripe. And in the spring the women of a family would make maple sugar together.

Dances were held in which only the women took part, and there were games which were played only by the women. The younger women played a very exciting ball game, and for the older women there were games of dice and chance. Each season was celebrated with special feasts and ceremonies.

There were no nearby grocery shops, and life, at times, could be very uncertain. But there was always a rhythm and pattern of life, and the joy of making and creating—of seeing the fruits of labor and of knowing that one's place in the group was an honored one.

There are many Indian women who justly deserve a place in this book, but who could not be included because of the limitations of space. The list would be quite a long one. The following, however, can be specially mentioned:

Dolly Akers (Assiniboin), the first Indian woman elected to the Montana Legislature and the first woman chairman of her tribal council.

Elizabeth Bender Cloud (Chippewa), "Mother of the Year" for 1950 and a distinguished worker for her people.

Amanda Crowe (Cherokee), an outstanding woodcarver and teacher of wood carving.

Alice Brown Davis (Seminole), chief of the Oklahoma Seminoles.

LaDonna Harris (Comanche), the wife of Senator Fred Harris from Oklahoma and a zealous worker in the Indian cause.

Ethel Brant Monture (Mohawk), a direct descendant of the famous Joseph Brant, Mohawk chief during the American Revolution, and a specialist in Mohawk history.

Buffy St. Marie (Cree), internationally known folk singer.

Gladys Tantaquidgeon (Mohegan), an anthropologist.

Te Ata (Chickasaw), internationally known lecturer.

Muriel Wright (Choctaw), historian for Oklahoma.

The **Yellowrobe** sisters, **Rosebud** and **Evelyn** (Sioux), Rosebud is an author and Evelyn a university medical lecturer.

WETAMOO

SQUAW SACHEM
OF POCASSET

It is mainly in colonial times that we find references to
Indian queens. Unfortunately, there is little information
about the women so designated unless they were involved in some particular way with the white settlers.

Wetamoo is one of these women. She was called Queen
Wetamoo by the English, and the Squaw Sachem of
Pocasset by her people. The word squaw comes from the
Narragansett tribe. It is part of a much longer word
meaning woman.

The word was understood by those tribes that were
members of the large Algonquin family. Others, however, were insulted when the word was applied to them
by colonists who did not realize that there were many
diverse Indian languages. Since the word came from an
enemy tongue, it must have a belittling meaning, it was
reasoned. As white men put the word into use, the term
squaw spread from one end of the country to the other.
It referred definitely to women, but in time it began to
be applied in a way that was insulting. Indian women

13

do not like the word today and object to being called by it.

In Wetamoo's time, however, the word squaw was perfectly respectable. A squaw sachem was a woman chief.

Wetamoo was a Wampanoag Indian. She was married to Wamsutta, the oldest son of Chief Massasoit. Her sister was married to the younger son, Metacom, one of the most remarkable Indians in history.

Massasoit was the great sachem of the Wampanoags whose thirty villages were scattered through Rhode Island and Massachusetts. He was the first and true friend of the Pilgrims, aiding them in many ways. At their first meeting, he gave them many miles of land for a pair of knives, a copper chain, and a pot of "strong water."

Indians, then, had no need for money. They did not know what it was, and they had no way to use it. But knives and axes, iron kettles for cooking, and other items of metal were valued highly. Such things Indians did not have, nor could they make. It is easy to see how a sharp knife would appeal to someone who had only a stone one.

Actually, the Indians did not realize that by accepting goods they were selling land at a price. They understood nothing of selling or buying. There was so much land and room for all. They believed that they were being given gifts for which they said "make use of the land. It is the creation of the Great Spirit for man to live upon." This misunderstanding on the Indians' part was very much to the advantage of the white man who could accumulate much land and then order the Indians away when he had strength in numbers.

Through other meetings, the Pilgrims and the Wampanoags became warm, firm friends. Massasoit protected the small settlement from attacks by hostile Indians. He taught the colonists all he knew about how to live

in the wilderness. He wrapped his mantle of chieftainship around the people of Plymouth and the colony
prospered.

The Pilgrims, too, helped the great sachem when he
was besieged by the Narragansetts. The sound and the
fire of their guns frightened off the attackers, even
though they were larger in number. As Indians eventually lost their fear of the "thunder stick," the gun became the most wanted possession they could have. The
tribe that had guns had power, and at first the settlers
were reluctant to place guns in Indian hands. For one
thing, they did not have that many guns to trade. For
another, guns could be turned against them.

When Massasoit became seriously ill and was thought
to be dying, the Pilgrims restored him to health. For
this, he believed that he owed them his life and never
would listen to words against them.

The Pilgrims treated Massasoit as if he were a king
and said that King James of England was his brother.
They gave his sons the names of Alexander and Philip,
calling them princes and treating them as though they
were the sons of royalty.

A treaty of friendship was drawn up with Massasoit
which was to last forty years. It provided that the Pilgrims and the Wampanoag Indians would not hurt each
other. If the treaty was broken by either side, the offend-
ing person would be punished by the Pilgrims. If either
group was attacked, the other would come to its aid.

It was with Massasoit and his people that the colonists
celebrated their first Thanksgiving feast. Among Indian
tribes, thanksgiving feasts were customary. There was
not just one, but often as many as twenty-four in a year.
So the Indians understood what the Thanksgiving feast
was all about. They entered into the spirit of the occa-
sion willingly. It was a further expression of friendship.

Against this backdrop Wetamoo grew up to young

womanhood. As Alexander's wife, she was not unknown to the people of Plymouth. It is probable that the young couple were feted at Plymouth at the time of their marriage. The colonists said that Wetamoo was graceful and lithe of figure and that she had a sensitive, lovely face.

She loved to be thought beautiful and she spent much time in adorning herself. The Wampanoags painted their bodies and faces in various colors, and at one dance, Wetamoo's face was painted a brilliant red. She had her hair powdered as the English ladies did.

Her arms, from wrists to elbows, were covered with bracelets. Around her neck were many necklaces of wampum and there were several kinds of "jewels" in her ears. She wore a kersey coat covered with wampum and girdles of wampum about her waist. She wore good white stockings and red shoes. She was not to be outdone by anyone.

That Wetamoo wore so much wampum was not merely a matter of adornment, however. It was a certain indication of her important status. Only the greatest sachems had them sewn on their buckskin shirts, moccasins, and leggings. Wrist bands and collars were woven from wampum as well as necklaces and belts.

Its chief use was to record agreements and bind contracts. A belt of white wampum exchanged by two tribes meant that peace had been declared. If the belt were stained red, it was a declaration of war.

Sachems were often honored with the presentation of a deep collar of wampum that draped down around his shoulders. Since Wetamoo is described as wearing much wampum, she had to be one who was thought of very highly.

Massasoit's sons did not share their father's feelings for the Pilgrims. They saw that the settlers were taking liberties with Indian land and that many injustices had taken place. When Indians did something wrong, they were speedily punished, but the Pilgrims were not punished for committing the same wrongs.

Alexander and Philip spoke to Massasoit about these things. But he was now an old man and his strength was failing.

"I spread a blanket for them to sit upon," he told his sons. "They saved my life. I pledged my word and my honor as a Wampanoag to remain their friend. I will not go against it."

"Now it takes many blankets for them to sit upon, and it will take many more," the two sons answered. "They do not ask the Wampanoags to sit with them, only to move farther away from where they sit. Soon there will be no place for us at all."

When Massasoit died, Alexander became "king." The English were soon disturbed by reports that he was plotting with the Narragansetts against them. He was asked to come to Plymouth to answer to these charges. Enraged that the English would order him about, Alexander refused to leave his lodge. The Pilgrims then sent soldiers to arrest him, and he was forced to go with them.

On the way to Plymouth, Alexander became ill and could walk no further. He was burning with fever and with fury at the high-handed behavior of the English. Wetamoo, who was with him, insisted that he be allowed to return home. She had his braves make a litter to carry him. But as he rested on the shore of the Taunton River, waiting for the litter to be finished, he died.

Wetamoo was overcome with grief. She wept bitterly and cried that Alexander had been poisoned. She promised that she would avenge him, that the English would suffer for the death of her husband.

Philip was now king, and plans against the English could still go forward in secret. Back and forth went the Wampanoag messengers—to the Narragansetts, to the Niantics, to the Nipmuks, and to the far-away Abenakis. For nine years, Philip worked, planned, and negotiated with the other tribes. He formed a strong confederacy as he continued to mingle with the colonists, even swearing that he was a subject of the king of England.

The colonists were increasingly arrogant and aggressive. They were able to produce their own food and the Indians were little needed in their economy, although their lands were coveted. Each continued to adopt something from the other. Indian words found their way into the English tongue, and Indian cookery into the diet of the settlements. There were dances and social activities.

The Indians now had muskets, and better than that, had learned how to make them. They had their own gunsmith forges hidden in the forests, and some of the war leaders even wore English armor.

So Philip bided his time and committed his people to pay one hundred pounds a year in tribute money to Plymouth. In spite of the surface easiness, the Indians understood that war was to come, and the impending struggle was also sensed by the colonists.

Strangely, Wetamoo did not marry Philip after her husband's death. Among her people it was customary for a man to marry his brother's widow, for it was his duty to assume responsibility for her care and protection. But Wetamoo returned to her home village of Pocasset where she became the squaw sachem. She married Quinipin, a nephew of the chief of the Narragansetts. This was perhaps a wise political move. When Philip was ready to begin warfare, he would need the help of this important tribe. Through Quinipin, Wetamoo could strengthen their loyalty.

Wetamoo was an able leader. The braves of her village

followed her gladly and it is said fought more valiantly under her than under any other leader. And many were the messengers that went from her lodge to that of the Wampanoag king. The squaw sachem had not forgotten her vow of vengeance. She was among those who pressed Philip the hardest to wipe out the English settlements.

When the day came and Philip finally struck, the colonists suffered heavy losses. Wetamoo joined him at once, bringing 300 braves and much food. With her men, she fought like a panther. Things went so well for the Indians at first that they felt certain of success although there were more than fifty thousand settlers in New England and Philip had only twenty thousand warriors. The Indians fought in their traditional way—a sudden attack, usually at dawn, then swift retreat to attack in another place. Although the Indians were now armed with guns they did not understand the white man's military tactics. Town after town was burned, however, and hundreds were killed and much of New England was devastated. But it was not long before the tide began to turn and at last Philip and his warriors were driven into a swamp and surrounded.

As the bullets of the colonists slashed through the trees, Wetamoo made brushes of twigs and tied them about the men so they could move through the underbrush without being seen. She helped in the frantic rush to build rafts and canoes for escape as the pressure of the fighting mounted.

With only 26 of her 300 warriors left, Wetamoo, too, managed to escape from the battleground.

The Great Swamp Fight took place in December, 1675. This was the decisive battle of the war and from then on, things went badly for the Indians.

The following August, the English surrounded Wetamoo's camp and captured all that remained of the powerful Narragansetts. Again Wetamoo tried to escape by canoe. Bullets riddled the sides and as the canoe sank, she swam desperately. But the current was too wild and too strong. It swept over her and she was drowned. When her body was washed ashore, her head was cut off and sent to Plymouth where it was placed on a pole.

Six days later Philip was killed. He too was beheaded and his head placed on a pole and carried to Plymouth where it stood for nearly twenty years. His wife and son with other captured Indians were sent to the West Indies and sold as slaves.

The descendants of the Wampanoags and Narragansetts, who still remain in New England have not forgotten the battle in the great swamp. They have dedicated the spot as a shrine of brotherhood. Each year, on the fourth Sunday in September, a pilgrimage is made to the monument which stands there and during the ceremonies, the people circle the monument carrying flowers to form a living wreath.

In Virginia, living in the same period as Wetamoo, there was another Indian queen of historical prominence. This was Queen Anne, the widow of Totopotomoi, chief of the Pamunkey.

The Pamunkey were the largest tribe of the thirty or more that belonged to the confederacy of which Powhatan, the father of Pocahontas, was chief. In a peace treaty made with the English in 1642, it was required that the Indians should bring twenty beaver skins to the governor of Virginia each March to acknowledge their allegiance to the king of England.

When the beaver became extinct, the Pamunkey Indians were then required to bring a tribute of game, skins, or fish. The treaty is still being observed by the Pamunkey people who now bring their annual gifts to the governor of Virginia on Thanksgiving Day.

Totopotomoi, with one hundred of his warriors, was

killed while helping the English at Jamestown turn back invading Indians.

Queen Anne remained an important figure in Virginia history for forty years, yet little has been written about her.

When Nathaniel Bacon, a young planter, rebelled against the colonial government, Queen Anne was called upon to supply a force of warriors to assist in ending the rebellion.

She came to the council, dressed in Indian dress and bringing her son with her. She refused to cooperate, saying that for twenty years she had been neglected and denied the compensation promised for the death of her husband. When told that she would have better treatment, she did send the warriors and gave other assistance.

In return for this, she was sent a silver crown by King Charles II. It is engraved to the "Queen of Pamunkey."

POCAHONTAS

THE SAVIOR
OF JAMESTOWN

Pocahontas is one of the most beloved figures in American history, and one of the world's great women. Every school child knows the story of Pocahontas and John Smith, for whom she risked her young life. The story of her greater accomplishments for the colony of Jamestown are not so familiar.

Pocahontas was the daughter of Powhatan, the chief of the Powhatan confederacy which included the Pamunkey, Mattaponi, and twenty-eight others. These Indians had more than two hundred villages in the tidewater area of Virginia.

Powahatan was called Powhatan by the settlers who arrived at Jamestown. His real name was Wahonsonacock.

Powahatan is said to have had eleven wives with whom he had more than twenty sons and eleven daughters. Of all these, his favorite child was Pocahontas—a bright, merry little girl whose name meant "Bright Stream Between Two Hills." She had another secret name—Matoax, "Little Snow Feather"—which was never used, except among her own people. The Indians believed that harm would come to one whose name was known to other tribes.

When the colonists arrived in 1607, they called the place where they would settle Jamestown, in honor of King James. During the first month of their arrival, a fort was built. Indians watched uneasily as the men cut down trees with axes such as they had never seen before and as they hunted with guns that made a loud and frightening noise. The Indians wanted these things badly, and finally they indicated that they would be peaceful and offered hospitality to the English.

The settlers, however, were fearful and mistrusting. They felt their lives were in danger from the Indians and they refused to put down their guns.

One of the leaders at Jamestown was Capt. John Smith. As he made trips about the country in search of food for the colony he visited many Indian villages and met with the Indians. The stories of these visits were carried back to Powhatan; and Pocahontas, as she sat by her father, heard them, too. She heard much about the white people and their wonderful fire-sticks.

In the winter, the food supply at Jamestown grew very low and the people suffered from hunger and cold. John Smith then set out to trade with the Chickahominy villages for corn. On the way, he was ambushed, taken captive and held in the village of Opechancanough, Powhatan's brother. Powhatan was inclined to be friendly to the whites, but his brother hated them with a deadly hate. He would have killed them all.

A number of weeks after his capture Smith was taken to Powhatan. He was marched down an aisle of flaming torches with rows of men on either side. Behind the men stood the women of the village. Smith was given water and fed while Powhatan, who was seated on a couch of boughs covered with raccoon skins, and his council discussed what would be done with him.

Then, several large stones were placed on the ground in front of Powhatan. Smith was dragged forward and his head was placed upon them. Over him stood a tall warrior with a club, which he swung high in the air, ready to smash out Smith's brains.

Suddenly there was a cry. Pocahontas dashed from the crowd and threw herself across Smith's body. She pleaded that his life be spared. She placed her own head upon Smith's to protect him. She was then only twelve years old.

At first, Powhatan was very angry. But, he could not deny his favorite daughter for it was the custom that a woman of the tribe could adopt a prisoner if she desired. Even so, this act took a great deal of courage, for she was not yet a woman and the temper of the men was one of hatred.

Powhatan agreed to let Smith return to Jamestown, but demanded from him two guns and a grindstone. For this, he said, he would give Smith a certain amount of land and forever honor him as his son, Nataquod.

Smith remained in Powhatan's village for a month. He was the almost constant companion of Pocahontas and between them grew a deep and abiding friendship. Pocahontas never tired of hearing about the people in Jamestown and in England, and Smith taught her how to speak English. He carved little trinkets for her and made her bracelets of coral.

When Smith eventually returned to Jamestown, he did not send the requested guns to Powhatan, but he did send other presents.

A year or so later, the fort and village at Jamestown were nearly destroyed by fire. Again there was no food, and Powhatan sent a party of Indians with twenty tur-

keys to help the settlers. However, he demanded twenty swords in return. When these were refused, he took back his gift and attacked Jamestown. When his braves were defeated, with many taken prisoner, he sent another party to the colony, accompanied by Pocahontas. He asked for forgiveness and for the release of those captured, and he sent baskets of bread and other food.

From then on, there was peace. Pocahontas went many times to the fort, sometimes alone and sometimes with a group of maidens, always bringing food in great quantity. The food she brought saved the lives of the desperate people.

In the fall of 1608, Captain Smith invited Powhatan to Jamestown to be honored and to be crowned king. But Powhatan refused to leave his village, saying that he was a king and that he would not leave his land.

Smith and a group of other colonists then decided to hold a coronation ceremony where Powhatan lived. The ceremony took place under a great tree on the steep bank of a river and to this spot was brought a bedroom set, other furniture, and a pitcher and basin—gifts for Powhatan.

Powhatan accepted a scarlet cape, but being completely unacquainted with English ceremonial customs, he would not kneel to receive the crown. Smith's soldiers then grasped him by the shoulders while others pushed behind his knees to force him into the proper position. When the crown was placed on his head, a ceremonial gun salute was fired. The shots frightened Powhatan and, expecting attack, he tried to flee. When he finally was convinced no harm was intended he presided over a great feast. He asked that his old moccasins and deer skin mantle be taken to his new brother, King James. The bedroom set and other furniture were left under the great tree.

Winter set in and the settlers were again in a hard way

for food. Once more, Capt. Smith appealed to Powhatan. As he camped outside the village with his men, the answer came that there would be no food unless the men laid down their guns and came unarmed to Powhatan.

In the night, Pocahontas crept into Smith's camp and warned him to leave at once, for Powhatan intended to kill him and his men. She said it would mean her death, too, if her father discovered that she had been there.

Smith fled and some time later returned to England for care when he was badly burned by an explosion of gunpower. The story spread among the Indians that he had died and Pocahontas grieved for her friend. Powhatan was sorry, too. Smith was his adopted son and he had a grudging admiration for him. He blamed the English for his death and a hatred for the colonists began to deepen. Pocahontas went no more to the fort until several years later when she intervened to save the life of another captive.

When Powhatan captured a group of colonists, kept them as prisoners, and confiscated their guns and tools, the English decided to use Pocahontas as a hostage. She was lured on board an English ship and taken to Jamestown, her first visit there in several years. Word was sent to her father that she would not be returned until he released the captured men, guns, and tools.

Three months later Powhatan sent the men back and asked for Pocahontas in exchange. The English refused until Powhatan delivered the rest of what he held.

While Pocahontas was a hostage of the English, she lived in the home of a minister. She was treated kindly, given religious instruction, and went with the women of the family to church each Sunday. She became the first Virginia Indian convert and was named Rebecca. During the time she spent in Jamestown she met and fell in love with John Rolfe, a wealthy, aristocratic Englishman.

After some months, Pocahontas was sent by ship to Powhatan's village as peacemaker. When the delegation reached their destination, they were met by 400 fully armed warriors. A truce was declared and two of Pocahontas's brothers promised to persuade her father to ransom her and to enter into a firm peace. But Powhatan stubbornly refused and Pocahontas returned with the others to Jamestown.

In April, there was great rejoicing at Jamestown. Pocahontas and Rolfe were to be married. The settlers expected the marriage to bind the English and the Indians together in a way that nothing else could do.

Powhatan refused to come to the wedding, but he did give his consent, and he sent his daughter's uncle and two of her brothers to the wedding. He also sent his daughter a pearl necklace as a wedding gift. The Rolfes built a home on the James River, where John had a tobacco plantation, and where their son, Thomas, was born.

Two years after their marriage, Pocahontas went to England with her husband and child. Powhatan was saddened at the parting. His merry little girl was now a grown woman with a child of her own. She had left her people for these Englishmen and now she would leave her country and go across the ocean. He sent one of his councilmen along with instructions to notch a stick as a count for every English person that he saw and report the numbers back to the chief. The Indian soon grew weary of this task and threw away his stick. He told Powhatan that the English were like the leaves on the trees. Counting them was quite impossible.

In England, Pocahontas was the center of attention. She carried herself like the daughter of a king and she soon adjusted to the manners and customs of her husband's family. She lived in a fine manor and was feted by society. Called the Lady, and sometimes the Princess,

Rebecca, she was received at court and was a great favorite of the king and queen. A portrait of her painted in court dress shows a beautiful young woman of great dignity. Her features are Indian and her expression pleasant and not at all unhappy. Her eyes are dark and searching.

Pocahontas had not been in England long when she was again reunited with John Smith. He called upon her when she was visiting friends, and the shock almost overcame her. It was several minutes before she could trust herself to speak. All the years she had thought Smith dead he had been alive, and now he stood before her.

Not long after this meeting with Smith, Pocahontas' health began to fail. She grew wan and thin. Then John Rolfe was appointed secretary and recorder-general for the Virginia colony, and it was time to return home. As the Rolfes waited in Gravesend to board ship, Pocahontas became gravely ill. Some said she had pneumonia, but it was more likely that she was afflicted with tuberculosis. Realizing that she would die, she said that all must sometime die and she rejoiced that her child lived.

With those words, Pocahontas expired. She was only twenty years old. She was buried in the yard of St. George's Parish Church, an ancient medieval church at Gravesend. There are several memorials to her in England including a statue and a stained glass window in St. George's. In Jamestown, there is also a statue memorializing Pocahontas, inscribed with these words: "She, next under God, was the instrument to preserve this colony from death, famine and utter confusion." The statue is of a young Indian girl in fringed buckskin dress, her hands outstretched in a gesture of friendship.

John Rolfe returned to America, but the boy, Thomas, was raised in England. It was John who advanced the growth and export of tobacco, giving to Virginia a tremendous source of revenue. But tobacco, itself, was the gift of the Indians who raised it long before the white man came. It is a purely American crop. Powhatan kept the peace with the colony, but after his death, Opechancanough, long hostile to the English, attacked with a large body of Indians. In the massacre that took place, John Rolfe was killed.

When Thomas Rolfe was a young man of twenty, he returned to Virginia, the land of his birth. The Indians had not forgotten that Pocahontas had left a son. To them, he was a kinsman, and the descendant of their great chief. When he arrived in the colony, he found awaiting him the plantation on which he was born and thousands of acres of land inherited from his grandfather, Chief Powhatan—about twelve hundred acres along the James River and extending a mile or so inland from a high bluff opposite Jamestown, and other large tracts scattered within a twenty-five-mile radius of the colony.

Like his father, Thomas became a tobacco planter. So strained were the relations between the colonists and the Indians after the massacre in which John Rolfe was killed, that no one was permitted to speak or have any form of communication with the Powhatans. Thomas, however, petitioned and was granted permission to visit his Indian kinfolk. Having been raised as an Englishman, he found Indian life alien to him, and he participated in the affairs of the colony rather than those of the Indians.

Another "Pocahontas" lived in Alabama. This was Milly Hadjo Francis who was born in a Creek village in 1802. Her father, Hillis Hadjo, was a prosperous farmer who owned slaves to work his farm.

Milly, one of several girls, is described as exceptionally pretty. She was brought up in the Creek way, but she spoke English fluently. She learned to pound Indian corn as the other women did, and to cook sofkey and blue dumplings and other Indian food.

There was a stick-ball game field in the village and in the evenings, Milly with her friends would watch this exciting games. Sometimes other tribes or other villages came to play. The game was a favorite one with the Indians of the South.

Milly's father was an important man. The whites called him "the prophet." When the Creek leaders came to her home to talk with her father, Milly often listened. All were worried about the whites who were pushing their way into the Creek country and forcing back the Creek frontier.

Sometimes the Indians talked of Tecumseh, the great chief of the Shawnees who was trying to unite all of the tribes against the whites. One day, he came to Milly's village and a council was held. Tecumseh's forceful, persuasive words convinced the Creeks and they pledged to join with him, led by Hillis Hadjo. When the War of 1812 broke out between England and America, the Creeks chose that time to open their own war against the whites. It was a disastrous move. General Andrew Jackson's troops and their Cherokee allies badly defeated the Creeks and destroyed their towns, forcing Hadjo and his family, with others of the tribe, to flee to Florida.

From then on, there was continuous fighting back and forth. The English encouraged the Creeks to keep up their harassment of the Americans, but gave them little or no actual support. Hillis Hadjo finally went to England, hoping to secure English assistance so that his tribe could put forth greater effort. He was showered with honors and gifts, and given vague promises of help. Nothing ever came of them, for the English knew that the war was going badly for them and that nothing was to be gained through further fighting on their part.

In the summer of 1817, the Creeks captured Capt. Duncan McKrimmon, a member of the Georgia militia. He was tied to a stake and was to be tormented and shot.

When Milly heard the yells and shouts of the warriors, she ran to the place where McKrimmon was held, begging her father to let him go. Finally her pleas won him over. Hillis said, though, that McKrimmon must shave his head and that he must live with the tribe. Not long after, however, the young captain was ransomed and returned to the militia.

The following winter, Andrew Jackson invaded Florida. Hadjo, whose hiding place had been betrayed by McKrimmon, was taken prisoner and hanged with others of the Creek leaders. Several months later a starving, ragged band of Creek women with their children, sought help at the army post. Milly, her mother, and her sister were among them.

McKrimmon, who was at the fort, had not forgotten that Milly had saved his life. He did all that he could to make things easier for her, and he asked her to marry him.

Milly refused his proposal. She did not want to be married out of gratitude. She would have done as much for any other captive. She returned to Creek country with her family and did not see McKrimmon again.

At the war's end, the government insisted that the Creeks must move west of the Mississippi to land that would be set aside and held as the home of all of the southeastern tribes. The new land was called Indian Territory. The government policy in this respect was inflexible and the Creeks had no choice but to go. They made their desperate journey in winter time. The suffering of the people was terrible and a good part of the people died on the way.

Milly Francis went with the rest of the Creeks. Fourteen years later she was found living near the present city of Muskogee, Oklahoma. She had been married and was widowed. Of her eight children, only a son and a daughter were living.

Milly, who dressed in a mixture of white and Indian fashion, was still a most attractive woman. She lived in great poverty and found it very difficult to support her children.

When this was reported to Washington, Congress voted her a medal and a payment of ninety-six dollars a year for her services in saving the life of McKrimmon. In those days, that was a goodly sum of money and would have greatly eased her life. Four years went by, however, before she was told of it, and by then her living conditions were even more wretched and she was dying of tuberculosis. She received the news joyfully, but she died before the medal and money reached her.

There is a monument to Milly Francis on the campus of Bacone College near Muskogee, a college for Indians first founded by the Creeks and now an integrated junior college.

MARY MUSGROVE
MATTHEWS BOSOMWORTH

INDIAN EMPRESS

Mary, whose Indian name was Coosaponakeesa, was born in 1700 in the Creek town of Coweta, Alabama. The Creeks, a large and powerful tribe, sprawled over Alabama and Georgia. They were divided into the "Upper" and "Lower" Creeks and Mary was related to the leading chiefs of both divisions. From childhood Mary was referred to as a princess by both the English and the Creeks.

One of the most famous of Indian women in colonial times, Mary held an extremely important place in the history of Georgia.

An unusually bright child, when she was seven she was taken to South Carolina to be educated. She was baptized in the Church of England and given religious instruction.

But Indian people did not thrive well when transplanted from the free life of the forest. Mary was no exception. She pined away from homesickness and finally ran back to her Creek people.

As she grew up, the Creeks and the South Carolina

colonists were at war. There were constant acts of hostility. Finally, Col. John Musgrove was sent by the Carolina government to bring about a treaty of peace.

The colonel's son John accompanied him to Coweta where he met Princess Mary. At sixteen she was pretty, lively, and for an Indian girl, not at all shy. She bore herself in a royal manner and soon attracted the young Englishman. The two were married and stayed among Mary's people for a number of years. When their only child was born, they moved to South Carolina where they lived quite happily.

Then, in 1732, the Musgroves moved to Georgia. John opened a large trading establishment on the top of Yamacraf Bluff, overlooking the Savannah River. He treated the Indians fairly, and because of his marriage to Princess Mary had great influence over them. He and Mary several times saved the lives of the colonists by warning them of approaching Indian attacks.

The trading post prospered. Merchandise from tradesmen in Charleston was distributed, and more than twelve hundred pounds of Indian deerskins cleared through the post each year. The Musgroves lived on a small but good plantation where they raised food crops. John became a very wealthy man.

In 1733, Gen. James Oglethorpe came to establish the colony of Georgia. Mary was among the first to greet him and he was greatly impressed by her marked intelligence. Since she could speak both Creek and English fluently, as well as several other Indian languages, Oglethorpe appointed Mary his interpreter and negotiator with the Indians, paying her a salary of five hundred dollars a year. He always treated her as an honored friend, and she was warmly welcomed at his home. She interpreted all of Oglethorpe's speeches to the Indians and helped in the drawing up and settling of treaties.

Largely because of Mary, the Creeks remained friendly

to the English. The tribe stood firm between the southern colonists and the Spaniards in the wars that took place in the struggle for control of the new world. It was due to Mary and her Creek people that the land above Florida did not become a Spanish possession.

When Oglethorpe needed a listening post closer to the Florida border, the Musgroves opened another trading station known as Mount Venture at the forks of the Altamaha River. It was here that John Musgrove died.

Mary later married another Englishman, Jacob Matthews, captain of the twenty rangers stationed at Mount Venture. From this post Mary rallied the Creeks to join with the Georgians in the war that finally broke out with Spain. Many of the Creek warriors went with Oglethorpe when he attacked Saint Augustine and Mary's brother was among those killed in the battle.

The Matthews left the outpost and went to Savannah in 1742, because Jacob was in ill health.

Governor Oglethorpe, who left Georgia the following year, gave Mary parting gifts of a diamond ring and a large sum of money as proof of his esteem and friendship.

Jacob Matthews died soon after Oglethorpe's departure. Despite the death of her husband, Mary remained loyal to the Georgia colony. Both the French and the Spaniards were attempting to win the Creeks to their side, but Mary's influence was stronger.

At forty-nine, still a handsome woman, Mary married Thomas Bosomworth, a clergyman of the Church of England and chaplain to Oglethorpe's regiment of Highlanders. Bosomworth was not a very pious man but, rather, an unprincipled fortune hunter. Through his marriage to Mary, he was appointed agent to the Creeks for the government of South Carolina.

An ambitious man, Bosomworth gave up his clerical duties to embark on a cattle raising program. But he was not practical and soon was heavily in debt to the colony for the grazing of his large herds. He was also in debt for the herds, for he had bought them on credit. In desperation, he involved Mary in a scheme to save him from ruin.

He prevailed upon her to secure from the Creeks a grant of three coastal islands—St. Catherine's, Ossabaw, and Sapelo. He also convinced her to ask for a grant to the tract of land near Savannah, which had been reserved by treaty to the Creeks for hunting. She said that all of this land had been a gift to her from the Creek chief, Tomichichi, a number of years before.

Bosomworth next pursuaded his wife to title herself empress of the Creeks. His hold over Mary was not a good one. He influenced her to actions that were against her interests and those of her people. He placed his unpaid for herds of cattle on St. Catherine's island.

Mary, at Bosomworth's bidding, then sent word to the colonists that she was claiming these lands and a large payment for her past services. She said that she was the sovereign ruler of the Creeks and was no longer a subject of the king of England.

"If my claims are not recognized," she wrote, "I will wipe out the colony when I arrive at Savannah with my warriors."

Gathering together a large force of Creek warriors, Mary advanced on the terrorized city. The people prepared to defend themselves. As the Indians approached, they were met by a troop of cavalry. Before they could enter the city, they were made to put down their weapons.

The procession of chiefs and a throng of yelling, angry braves, painted for war, was led by Bosomworth and Empress Mary. Bosomworth was dressed in his churchly robes, and Mary in Indian clothing.

The Indians were received by the president of Savannah and members of the city council. A welcoming artillery salute of fifteen guns was fired. Nobody looked afraid, although there were more Indians than colonists. To show fear would have been disastrous. The situation was very dangerous, for the slightest action or word that might be misunderstood could trigger off complete destruction.

A council was held which lasted for several days. All the chiefs spoke at length in the Creek language which then had to be interpreted for the colonists. Then the speeches of the colonists had to be put into the Creek tongue. Mary and Bosomworth incited the Indians to make angry and threatening remarks and built up tension. Finally, they were both placed in jail and told they would be held there until they promised good behavior.

Meanwhile, the council went on. All of the chiefs were given presents, and at last they were brought to a calmer state of mind. Although the English had begun the use of royal titles among the Indians, they reminded the Creeks that such titles belonged to the royal families of Europe. Mary had no royal blood and the Creeks had no royal families. Her titles were all assumed. This the Creeks had to admit. Recognizing that Mary's claims were not truthful and that they were being used by Bosomworth, they decided to return home.

Bosomworth stormed and raged and Mary stamped her feet and screamed. She promised death to all whites and insisted that the lands were hers. She and her husband were finally allowed to go to England to plead their cause.

After many years in the law courts, the Bosomworths were given a royal grant to the island of St. Catherine's and they were allowed to sell the other two islands to the colonists.

From then on, the Bosomworths lived quietly on St. Catherine's. Mary devoted herself to strengthening the ties of friendship between the Creeks and the English until her death in the early 1760s. She is buried on the island.

NANCY WARD

BELOVED WOMAN
OF THE CHEROKEES

The Cherokees were one of the great and powerful tribes of the southeastern part of this country. They held sway over a vast forest area in the area that was to become the states of Virginia, West Virginia, North and South Carolina, Georgia, Alabama, and Tennessee. Their friendship was eagerly sought by the English, French, and Spaniards who were struggling to gain control of the New World.

Nancy Ward's uncle, Chief Atakullakulla, was taken to England with others of the tribe and treated royally. He was so won over that he pledged allegiance to King George I, and the king agreed to provide the Indians with trade goods, guns and ammunition, and material for clothing.

With English axes, the Indians could cut down trees instead of laboriously burning them down, which had been their only way of clearing ground. It was not long before the Cherokees were living in log houses as the English did. More and more they took on the ways of

39

the white men and grew accustomed to the comforts and luxuries of white living.

Nancy's home was at Chota, in southern Tennessee near the present city of Knoxville. Chota was an important village dating back to ancient times. Her Cherokee name was Nanye-hi, a very old one meaning "One Who Goes About." It was a legendary name, related somehow to the Spirit People. The settlers said they changed this name to Nancy, which was easier for them to say.

When Nancy was very young, she married a brave named Kingfisher, with whom she had two children—a son, Fivekiller, and a daughter, Catherine. The use of both Indian and English names indicates the change that was taking place. The English influence was overlaying Indian thought and habit and the new patterns reflected both cultures.

Further to the south, in Georgia and Alabama, were the Creeks, another large and strong tribe. They were longtime enemies of the Cherokees, but like the Cherokees, they were also friends of the English. Like the Cherokees, too, the Creeks reflected the incoming white culture. They learned about slavery from the Southern planters, and had Negro slaves themselves. Indians often used captives as slaves if they did not put them to death or adopt them into the tribe. But slavery was not an institution among Indians until it was brought in from the outside world.

There was continual fighting between the Creeks and the Cherokees, and in one of these battles Kingfisher was killed. Nancy was at his side during the fierce battle. She chewed the ends of bullets for her husband so that they would be ragged and cause serious, tearing wounds. When Kingfisher fell, she sprang from the fallen log where she was hidden and snatched up his rifle. Fighting as hard and as courageously as the men, she helped to bring about the defeat of the Creeks.

When the battle was over, the Cherokees divided their spoils. Some of the Negro slaves had fought with their Creek owners, and one of these was given to Nancy. This made her the first Cherokee owner of a black slave and she was responsible for introducing her people to slavery as it was used in the South.

After this battle, Nancy was also given her title of Beloved Woman, which made her a person of great influence. As Beloved Woman, she was head of the Council of Women of her tribe, and this gave her a vote in the Chief's Council. It gave her other rights, too. She could decide the fate of any captive and she could speak her opinion and that of the other women on all matters of tribal concern.

Nancy stood for peace rather than war, although she had fought as bravely as any warrior in Indian battles. As she saw more and more white men coming into Cherokee country and hemming in the Cherokees, she believed that they had no choice but to try to learn the ways of white people. It was best to live together in good will, she said, and many times she befriended the frontier settlers.

A few years after the death of Kingfisher, Nancy married Brian Ward who had come to America from Ireland. He was a trader among the Cherokees and had fought against the English in the French and Indian Wars. Perhaps it was through him that Nancy formed her feelings of friendship for the Americans.

Not much is known of this marriage except that there was one child, Elizabeth. Brian did not stay long after his daughter was born. He returned to his home in South Carolina where he was married to a white woman. It is said that Nancy and Elizabeth often visited him and were treated with great respect by the Ward family.

Those who knew Nancy then described her as tall, erect, and beautiful, with long, silken black hair and large, dark eyes. She had a stately bearing and a proud, but kindly, manner. Although she had no formal education, she was of superior intelligence and character.

As time went on, the English became divided among themselves with some of the colonists threatening to break away from the mother country. This unrest, of course, was known to the Indians and an even greater effort was made by the English to hold their loyalty.

Chief Dragging Canoe, who was a son of Atakullakulla, and his followers were armed by the English and asked to attack the settlements in order to put down the rising tide of dissension.

When Nancy heard of this, she sent a secret warning to the settlers so that they could prepare to defend themselves from the coming invasion. One of the settlers, a Mrs. William Bean, was captured and brought to the Indian camp to be put to death. She was taken to the top of a mound, tied to a stake, and wood heaped around her ready for lighting.

But Nancy exercised her right as Beloved Woman. She refused to allow the death of Mrs. Bean and the warriors had to obey and set her free.

Mrs. Bean lived with Nancy until it was safe to travel. Then she was placed in the care of Nancy's son and brother and returned to her family. In the meantime, the grateful woman taught Nancy how to make cheese and butter. Nancy was the first among her people to buy a cow.

Nancy helped the settlers frequently, saving the lives of a number of captives. There were other incidents of hostile actions where she was an effective appeaser. As unrest continued among the Indians, the Americans struck against them in full measure for their loyalty to the English and for their attacks upon American settlements. In order to break the English hold, they had to break the strength of the Cherokees, too.

Nancy was sent by the chiefs to meet the advancing American troops under Col. Arthur Campbell and to negotiate for peace; she was unsuccessful. The Cherokee country was laid waste, more than a thousand cabins were burned, and fifty thousand bushels of corn were destroyed. But Nancy's relatives, when captured with other Cherokees, were treated with courtesy as a mark of respect for the Beloved Woman. Her village of Chota was not destroyed.

After the frightful years of the war, George Washington was determined that there would be no more fighting. Attention had to be turned to building the country, and the Indians, too, must restore themselves. The Cherokees were the first tribe to pledge allegiance to the United States at the war's end. They were the first tribe to sign a treaty with the United States.

A peace commission was appointed to meet with them in South Carolina in 1785. Nancy spoke for her badly defeated people. Still a stately and beautiful person, she made a tremendous impression. To indicate her important standing in the tribe, she was introduced with the presentation of strings of wampum to the peace commissioners.

Nancy spoke of her delight that the peace council was taking place and that the Great White Father had good thoughts for his Red Children.

"I hope that you have now taken us by the hand in real friendship," she said. "I have borne and raised up warriors. I am now old, but hope yet to bear children who will grow up and people our Nation now that we are under the protection of Congress and shall have no more disturbance. The young warriors rejoice that we have peace and hope that the chain of friendship will never be broken."

She brought to the conference a pipe and some tobacco so that the pipe of peace could be smoked to seal the friendship. Tobacco, to the Indians, was a sacred plant. It was believed that the smoke, rising toward the sky, carried the prayers of the people to the Great Spirit. When the pipe had been smoked, an agreement could not be broken.

Whites participated in the peace pipe ceremony thinking it merely a ritual. They did not truly understand the deep spiritual significance or symbolism that it had for Indians.

For a while, all went well. The Cherokees made rapid progress in the ways of civilization. They had their own farms, a weaving industry, their own schools, could read and write in their own language, and had their own newspaper published in the Cherokee alphabet invented by Sequoya. They were the only tribe to have their own written language.

Many of the men owned large tracts of land and kept Negro slaves to cultivate them. They were as wealthy as the white slave owners surrounding them, and they were as highly cultured. Indian ways and customs were lost as they lived more and more like white people.

Nancy, too, had become wealthy. She had opened an inn on the Ocowee River near the Georgia border which was a popular stopping place for travelers. She had slaves and livestock and a home that was comfortably furnished. With her children and grandchildren, she continued to be an influence for good. The settlers affectionately greeted her as "Granny" Ward, for she was now elderly but still of striking appearance. And she still dreamed of lasting peace and friendship.

But her dream was not to last. As the years went by, the settlers began to resent the Indians and to crowd them, and to press for their lands. The government then decreed that all Indians were to be removed west of the

Mississippi River to Indian Territory, which would be theirs—"forever"—without interference.

Some of the Cherokee leaders thought it best to go, foreseeing only increased tension leading to serious trouble. Others refused to listen to talk of leaving. "It is our country," they said. "We will defend it, even if we die."

In 1817, a great council was held to discuss the further cession of Cherokee land and the removal to the west. Nancy was not able to attend, for she was too old to make the journey. She sent her walking cane to symbolize that she was relinquishing her high office as Beloved Woman, and she sent her vote on several questions, especially on the removal to the west.

She addressed the men of the council as warriors. She begged that they not agree to move. "Cherokee mothers do not wish to go to an unknown country," she said. "We have raised all of you on the land we now have, which God gave us to inhabit. We have understood that some of our children wish to go over the Mississippi, but this act . . . would be like destroying your mothers. We beg of you not to part with any more of our land . . . but keep it for our growing children for it was the good will of our creator to place us there. . . . Continue on our land and enlarge your farms and cultivate and raise corn and cotton and we . . . will make clothing for you which our father the president has recommended to us."

But things had changed among the Cherokees. The traditional clan system had been discarded. The people had developed a republican form of government with a written constitution based on that of the United States, and in this they were again unique. The capital had been moved to New Echota, Georgia, where a legislature with an upper and lower house was established. What the Beloved Woman said no longer mattered.

With the discovery of gold in Georgia, the hue and

cry against the Indians rose to fever pitch. The Cherokees had learned to live with the white man and to be like the white man. They had become the white man's equal in the white way of doing things, as Nancy had so often advised.

If the discovery of gold had not taken place, matters might have worked out differently. But with that happening, the Cherokees were doomed.

Nancy did not live to see the sad day when her people were forced to march away from the homes and the land they loved, leaving everything behind them. She never knew of the terrible suffering that took place on the enforced journey still called the Trail of Tears. More than one-fourth of the Indians died and were buried along the way. The rest tried to begin anew in the alien country that was later to be taken from them again to become part of the state of Oklahoma.

When Nancy died, her family reported that a light rose from her body and flew away towards Old Chota, her home. She was buried on a hill in Benton, Tennessee, and her grave marked with a bronze tablet, placed there by the Nancy Ward Daughters of the American Revolution chapter. It reads "Princess and Prophetess of Tennessee. The Pocahontas of Tennessee and the Constant Friend of the American Pioneer."

SACAJAWEA

THE GIRL GUIDE

Though her name may not be familiar to everyone today, Sacajawea, the Shoshone girl who guided the Lewis and Clark Expedition to the Pacific coast, is one of the most honored women in American history. There are several statues of her, and a number of monuments have been placed along the trail that she traveled as well as on the site of her birthplace in Idaho. It is said that there are more statues and monuments to Sacajawea than to any other woman in this country.

When she was nearly fourteen years old, the Shoshones were attacked by the Hidatsas while they were preparing buffalo meat after a hunt. The Shoshones lived in the mountains, but they hunted on the plains, moving about after the buffalo herds.

Sacajawea was seized by her long, black hair and lifted to the back of a warrior's horse. As she was carried away, she saw her brother in the midst of the fighting. That was the last time she was to see her people for several years.

The Hidatsas kept Sacajawea as a slave, but she was

not treated unkindly. The women showed her how to plant corn—how to dig the soil with a pointed stick, how to push in the seeds, how to hoe the ground with a buffalo shoulder blade. When the crops were ripe, she helped with the havest. The fields of corn were a constant wonder, for her own people were nomads and did no planting. The round, earth lodges of the Hidatsas were a wonder, too. Sacajawea had always lived in a skin tipi and never in one place.

When she was about sixteen, she was sold to Touissant Charbonneau, a French trader. She was pleasing to the eye, young and strong, and she made a good wife.

In the winter of 1804, Lewis and Clark, with their men, arrived on the first lap of their long journey. They would rest through the rugged months until spring, getting supplies together and boats in order for the task ahead. Charbonneau was hired as an interpreter for the expedition and he decided that Sacajawea would go with him. She could still speak her own language, she knew the trails through the mountains, and a woman with the party would indicate to the tribes that this was a peaceful mission.

Sacajawea was eager to go. Perhaps she would see her people again. And she would see what lay on the other side of the mountains. A great ocean, the white men said. What was an ocean like?

Sacajawea's son, Baptiste, was born in February, and in April, the expedition started out. With her baby on her back, Sacajawea rode in the lead boat. Baptiste was carried in that fashion, held close and tight by his mother's blanket-shawl, for the whole of the journey of more than four thousand miles.

Sacajawea proved her value at once. Never did she voice a word of complaint, no matter how rough the way. She encouraged and inspired the men, cooking their meals, doing their washing and mending, and caring for them when they were sick. To a man, they all loved the gentle person whom they called Janey, the name given to her by Captain Clark.

She knew just where to find wild plants that would supplement the constant meat diet. Her sense of direction was unerring, and she remembered many places from her childhood. Because of her knowledge of the Hidatsa and Shoshone languages, she made it possible to communicate with tribes met along the way. At night, when they were camped she sat by Captain Clark and in a combination of sign language, halting French, and English told of Indian trails and villages, warned of bad water or poisonous plants.

Strong winds and rough waters fought the heavily laden boats forcing the expedition to move slowly. Once a boat filled with irreplacable instruments and valuable papers capsized. It was Sacajawea, Baptiste still on her back, who plunged into the icy water and swam about until she had saved everying. She was carried to a roaring fire on the shore, where the men gave her a hearty cheer. Sacajawea did not know why the things were so valuable, but Captain Clark was delighted that they had been saved, and that was all that mattered to her. She did not consider that she had done anything unusual.

As the expedition neared Sacajawea's homeland, the two leaders were worried. No white men had ever passed to the west of her people. Would the Shoshones recognize her, and would they listen to her?

When Sacajawea saw the Shoshone camp, she gave a cry of joy. The braves, with their chief, awaited the approach of the white men. Sacajawea rushed forward and threw her blanket around the shoulders of the chief.

"We are of one blanket," she cried, for the chief was her brother, Cameahwait.

There was great rejoicing over Sacajawea's return, and a council was held. Sacajawea spoke in behalf of Lewis and Clark while the Indians listened with close attention. She told of their great need for horses, for without them the party could not cross the Great Divide. She asked for guides to help them along the way.

The Shoshones gladly gave the expedition horses, and they provided a guide to help them get through the mountains to the navigable waters of the Columbia. The expedition did not leave the Shoshones until the end of August and the hardest part of the journey lay ahead of them. Winter storms were already swirling through the mountains, clogging the trails with snow and bombarding the expedition with sleet. Both horses and men were exhausted from the steep trails and it often seemed that they could not endure the hardships another day. The sight of the uncomplaining Sacajawea with her baby helped them to keep on.

Then, one November day, the flag was raised to the top of a tall tree, and Captain Clark, in sight of the ocean, claimed the land for the United States. The men stood in awed silence, and Sacajawea held Baptiste up to see the waves breaking on the shore. She was the first woman to cross the Great Rocky Mountains; because of her, the whole Northwest Territory would be opened up.

Captain Clark tried to tell her of his gratitude for all that she had done. Without her, he said, the expedition might never have succeeded. Sacajawea did not understand him. They had shared much together and now she wanted to share her own deep feelings. She smiled and pointed to the ocean and said, "I see! I see!" For her, that was enough.

On the return journey in 1806, Sacajawea guided the expedition through the mountain passes of Montana. What became of Sacajawea when the expedition was over is something about which historians disagree. There are confusing reports, but it is known that she and Charbonneau lived in St. Louis for a time. Captain Clark had formed a strong attachment for Baptiste and he assumed responsibility for his education. When he was eighteen, Baptiste was taken by Prince Paul of Württemberg to Europe and remained there for six years. On his return to the United States he spent many seasons trapping in the Rockies, saw service in the Mexican War, and spent eighteen years in the California gold fields.

The Shoshones insist that Sacajawea returned to her own people and lived on the Wind River Reservation in Wyoming, where she was joined by Baptiste and an adopted son, Bazil. Her grave is said to be in the Indian cemetery, marked with a simple tablet, and giving her age at death as close to one hundred years.

Sacajawea's name has several spellings and meanings. In Hidatsa, it means "Bird Woman," and in Shoshone, "Boat Woman." She was also known as "Lost Woman." Whatever her name, she has a firm hold upon the imagination of the American people and a firm place in their hearts.

Marie Dorion of the Iowas, was another, but lesser known woman guide who has a story of achievement similar to Sacajawea's.

Marie was the only woman on the famed overland expedition to Astoria (Oregon) in 1811–12. She, too, was a heroine of the trail, but little is known of her early life.

Marie's husband, Pierre Dorion, was a half-Sioux, half-French trader who was employed in the fur trade on the Missouri River. When he was asked to join the expedition to Astoria as an interpreter, he refused to make the trip without Marie and their two sons. Astoria was the new Columbia River fur depot established by John Jacob Astor.

The Astoria party left St. Louis in March, traveling up the Missouri by keel boat. They left the river near where the city of Pierre, South Dakota, now stands, and continued westward by land. Marie went on foot, sometimes carrying her younger child, two years old, on her back. Through the weeks of hardship she showed great force of character and won the respect of all the men.

When the party attempted to navigate the Snake River, they failed because of the treacherous current. So the journey went on as before, with many of the men falling out because of exhaustion. As they neared the present site of North Powder, Oregon, in December, Marie gave birth to her third child. The baby, a boy, lived only eight days.

It was not until February, 1812, that the party reached the end of their 3,500 mile trek. As trying as the experience had been, Marie's most severe ordeal was yet to come. About a year later, the Dorions left Astoria with a beaver trapping expedition. A cabin was built near the juncture of the Boise and Snake rivers, about 330 miles east of Astoria. From here, the men went out to trap.

In January, 1814, all of the men were massacred by hostile Indians. Overwhelmed with grief at first, Marie gathered what provisions she could, loaded them and her children on a horse, and set out for the Columbia River.

After nine days she had gone about 120 miles, when she was caught in a bad snowstorm in the mountains. She built a hut of branches, packing snow around it for warmth, and somehow managed to survive. She killed her horse for food and lived for fifty-three days in the most bitter weather in her precarious shelter.

By mid-March, her food and supplies were exhausted, so she set out once more. For three days, she wandered completely snow-blind. At last, weak with hunger and barely able to crawl, she stumbled onto a village of friendly Indians and was taken in by them. Her two sons, whom she had hidden nearby, were rescued by her new-found friends. Later she was taken to Fort Okanogon, a fur station in what is now western Washington.

Marie lived at Fort Okanogon with her second husband

for a number of years. She later married her third husband, Jean Baptiste Toupin, a French-Canadian interpreter at another trading post. By Toupin she had a son and a daughter, and her descendants still live in the Northwest.

In 1841, the Toupins settled on a farm in the Willamette Valley. Marie was sixty when she died, but her age was recorded as around one hundred. The sufferings that she had gone through must have aged her greatly in appearance. She was buried in the parish church not far from Salem, Oregon.

SARAH WINNEMUCCA

ARMY SCOUT

Sarah Winnemucca was a Paiute Indian. She was born in an area now part of the state of Nevada. Her people lived entirely unmolested by whites, for few traders or explorers came their way.

When the Paiutes saw white men for the first time, they were terrified of their bearded faces. Indians did not have any facial hair and they thought the whites looked like dogs.

As a child Sarah was terrified of whites, too. She screamed that they were owls, and at night she would lie awake thinking of their big white eyes surrounded by hair. It was not until a white woman nursed her back to health from a serious illness that Sarah overcame her fear, which had become a mania.

With the influx of more and more white people bad things began to happen. Furs were stolen from Indian traps and Indians were killed for sport. In turn, Indians plundered wagon trains following the California Trail.

Sarah was the second daughter of Chief Winnemucca, and the fourth of his nine children. Her grandfather, the first Chief Winnemucca, was said to have guided Capt. John C. Fremont across the Sierra-Nevada range to California in 1845–46. The whites called him Captain Truckee. He found the ways of the whites to his liking and took some of his people to work on a ranch in the San Joaquin Valley.

Sarah grew up a pretty, merry child. Her Indian name was Shell Flower. She would gather the blossoms of the flower for which she was named, weaving them into wreaths and necklaces. Then she would take part in the tribal Festival of Flowers. In this, the Paiute girls, all named for flowers, would sing about the flowers for which they were named. It was believed that they became flowers as they sang.

Because she was apt at speaking both English and Spanish, Sarah was chosen as companion to the daughter of the agent for a stage coach company and lived with this family for a year at the Mormon trading post. During that time she converted to Christianity, though without giving up her Indian faith, and became known as Sarah.

As her grandfather approached the end of his life, he begged that Sarah be sent to school. She was placed in St. Mary's Convent School at San Jose. She loved the school and was a good pupil, but some of the wealthy white families objected to having an Indian with their children. They forced the nuns to send her back to her people after three weeks.

By then, white settlers were coming into western Nevada in large numbers, creating serious troubles for the Indians. The Paiute War broke out in 1860 and ended with the Indians being placed on a reservation at Pyramid Lake not far from present day Reno. From then on, Indians suffered greatly. The appointed Indian agents were dishonest men who brought the Indians to starvation and destitution. They did nothing to help them adjust to the new way of life.

If hungry Indians stole cattle, soldiers retaliated by attacking the Indian villages when the men were away hunting. The women, children, and old people were killed without mercy. Sarah's baby brother was among the casualties and her mother and a sister also died later.

The poverty stricken Indians, without resources of any kind, flocked to the military post begging for rations. Sarah, who knew several Indian languages, was the post interpreter. In the frequent clashes between the Indians and the whites, she always tried to act as peacemaker. She hated the Indian agents and blamed them for the troubles of her people, but she tried to maintain peace because she knew that the Indians would suffer the most if hostilities broke out. She was loved by the settlers and the army respected her. Her own people, too, held her in high regard for they knew she would always try to help them.

Once, an Indian was shot by one of the post clerks who had ordered him to do something which he did not understand. The aroused Indians were determined that the storekeeper, too, must die. Sarah and her brother rode to his home in an effort to save his life. They warned him to leave. When he refused to do so, they returned to the Indians, explained what had happened, and finally succeeded in quieting them.

In 1872, the fortunes of the Paiutes changed somewhat for the better. They were placed on a new reservation in southern Oregon. At first, all went well. The agent was an honest man whom the Indians trusted. Sarah interpreted for him and she also taught in a school he opened for the children.

But then a new agent arrived who did not treat the Indians fairly. When Sarah reported his conduct, he ordered her off the reservation. Some of the other Paiutes were also leaving to join the Bannocks in Idaho who were ready to go on the warpath.

When the Bannock War broke out in June, 1878, Sarah offered her services to the army as scout and interpreter. She felt, with many of her people, that the army treated them fairly and would continue to do so. She volunteered to go as a scout to the Bannock camp when no man— white or Indian—would undertake this highly dangerous mission. When she learned that her father and some of his followers had been forced to join the Bannocks against their will and were being held by them, she begged that there be no attack until she had brought them to safety.

Sarah followed the trail of the Bannocks through rugged wilderness country from southwestern Idaho into eastern Oregon. She arrived near the camp on a dark, stormy night, and hastily dressed in Bannock clothing. The dark and the storm would serve her well.

On the way, she had heard that her brother was made to act as a sentry. Somehow she must find him. As she approached the camp, she gave a signal that she and her brother had used as children. She prayed that he would recognize it.

She repeated the signal again and again as she went from the cover of one thicket to another, from one rock to another, from one bush to another bush. It seemed hours before she heard an answering signal.

They must get their people away, Sarah told her brother when they were together. The army was coming and they would all be killed.

Silently they went into the camp where the Paiutes were in the center of the 325 Bannock lodges. Spiriting away their father and most of the Paiutes was no easy task.

Returning to the army base, Sarah was able to give

much valuable information about the Bannocks. She had covered the long distance by traveling almost constantly for three days and two nights, with no sleep and little to eat or drink. Her feat was worthy of the toughest soldier and all the army men acknowledged it. She continued to serve as scout and interpreter for Gen. O. O. Howard throughout the Bannock campaign and he was ever after her loyal friend.

When the war was over, the government ordered the Paiutes to the Yakima Indian reservation. The Bannocks were to be sent there also. Sarah pleaded for her people who had remained peaceful, and in this the army upheld her. But the plea fell on deaf ears. The Indians were told shortly before Christmas that they had a week to get ready for the trip across the mountains in the dead of winter. Overcoats were issued to the men but the women were given nothing. Sarah did what she could to get furs and clothes together for the women already shivering in the cold.

The Indians were months on their way to Washington. They had only fifty wagons, the temperature dropped below zero, and many died. Two babies that were born during the trip froze to death. The Paiutes were not expected in Washington and no plans had been made to receive them. When the agent learned of their coming, he was distraught. How do I care for them, how do I feed them without money? he wired Washington. Washington apparently did not know either, since there was no response. But in Oregon, a warehouse bulged with clothes and provisions, sent there by mistake, and not an Indian around!

The Yakimas put up a large building—the rudest kind of shelter—and in this the 543 Paiute people were housed. Their condition was one of extreme destitution. Some were literally naked. A school was opened and the children made good progress, but they had no clothes and no books.

The following winter, the people were still in pitiful shape. In an effort to help them, Sarah went to San Francisco to appeal for assistance. The Paiutes had not fought in the Bannock War, but they were now at the mercy of the Bannocks who hated them because of it, she explained. They should be returned to Oregon, she begged.

Those who heard her said she spoke with such emotion that many were moved to tears. She was given wide attention in the press. But those in power turned on her, slandering her and falsely accusing her of being of low character. She refused to be intimidated or turned aside by the evil things said of her. The needs of her people came first and injustice had to be righted.

What Sarah was saying finally made an impression; Sarah, her father, and others of the tribe were invited to come to the Capital at government expense to tell their story. They met with the secretary of the interior and also with President Hayes, who promised help.

They were given written orders that the Paiutes were to be returned to Oregon, and told that there would be immediate aid—food, clothing, and tents. But when Sarah returned home, none of these things were there. The snow was waist deep in the mountains, and it was a hazardous journey to the Yakima reservation. The agent had received no word from Washington, and he would not let Sarah tell the Indians that they were to be returned to Oregon. She had an order for her people's freedom but it was not worth the paper it was written on.

Disheartened, Sarah wrote to General Howard, who invited her to come and teach a school for Indian children at his army post. There she met and married Lt. L.

H. Hopkins who went east with her on a lecture tour on behalf of her people. None of the promises made by President Hayes had been kept, and the lands of the Paiutes in Oregon were being used by white stockmen.

Sarah spoke throughout New England, Pennsylvania, and Maryland and was warmly received. The pictures of her taken at that time show a pleasant-faced young woman with long, flowing hair. She was dressed in a buckskin dress trimmed with beads and shells. Because the newspapers referred to her as "Princess," she wore on her head a crimson crown set with brilliants.

During her travels, Sarah wrote a book called *Life Among the Paiutes,* a vividly written account of the sad saga of the Paiutes. The proceeds from the sales helped to finance the lecture tour.

Sarah was able to stir public opinion to such a degree that thousands of people signed petitions calling for the government to keep its promises to the tribe. Finally, Congress passed a bill to this effect, but the secretary of the interior refused to act upon it.

Friends in Boston raised the money for a small school and Sarah returned to teaching. She taught for three years although she was severely crippled with rheumatism and troubled with recurring fevers. Her last months were spent in failing health. She died from tuberculosis before she reached the age of fifty, worn down from her brave, but futile fight. While she failed to accomplish the things she set out to do, her life could not be described as a failure. She lived with no thought of self, but entirely in service to others.

WINEMA

THE PEACEMAKER

Winema's story is an unusually thrilling one. Two books and a play have been written about her, for she was a heroine of her time.

She was born near the California-Oregon border. Her father was the son of Chief Modocus of the Modocs. Her cousin was a Modoc chief known as Captain Jack. He, too, would stand out in history and Winema would risk her life by going against him. Together, they would write a chapter of courage that gave them an enduring place in the annals of time.

Because she had fine brown, or reddish hair, unlike the black hair of her people, Winema was called Strange Child. When she was still a very young girl, she earned the name Winema which means "Strong Hearted Woman," but is sometimes incorrectly interpreted as "Chief Woman."

She earned her name one day when she was canoeing with some of her playmates on Upper Klamath Lake. Her canoe was driven into the dangerous rapids of the river and it seemed that she would be swept to her death. Unafraid, she stood up in the boat and guided it past rough boulders that would have dashed it to pieces and into quiet waters. This was quite a feat for a young girl and the Indians marveled at her bravery. A few years later, when she was not quite fifteen, Winema again acted courageously in a crisis. The Modocs were surprised by a band of warriors from an enemy tribe. As they prepared to flee, Winema rallied the men into making a victorious stand.

When Winema was fifteen, she rejected the husband chosen for her—a Modoc youth named Uleta. Instead, she married Frank Riddle, a Kentucky miner whose life she had saved twice—once when he was threatened by the jealous Uleta, and once when he was cornered by a maddened she-bear. Winema flicked her calico skirt at the bear and drove it away with a torrent of Modoc words.

The happily married Riddles settled down to ranching. As Winema learned "white ways" from her husband, she taught them to her people. Though still in her teens, she was often looked to for help as tension mounted between the Indians and the whites. The Modocs felt themselves hemmed in by the settlers swarming into their country and Winema was frequently called upon to interpret as Indian anger intensified. She tried to keep peace and to build good relationships for she believed that all people were equal and should be treated as such. Many times she averted bloodshed and the Modocs generally trusted her. Captain Jack, too, was influenced by his young cousin, but he grew increasingly hostile. Then he began to stir up and deepen bad feelings between the Indians and whites.

Finally, a treaty was made with the Modocs and Winema was especially helpful in bringing about an agreement that was satisfactory to both people—all but Captain Jack. The Modocs were removed to the Klamath reservation in Oregon, but Captain Jack refused to stay there. He continued to roam over the country, fishing and hunting where he pleased.

There were other troubles almost from the start. The Klamaths were enemies of the Modocs, and they continued to be. They refused to let the Modocs cut timber or hunt game on their reservation and they made things quite miserable.

When Col. A. B. Meacham was named superintendent of Indian affairs in Oregon, the trouble was nearing its peak. Meacham was a fair man and he tried to help the Indians, especially the women. He issued orders to white men living with Indians that they must marry them or face prosecution.

Captain Jack grew more sullen and angry and more demanding that the Modocs be allowed to return to their home. But Meacham could not listen to such talk. An agreement had been made and the Modocs must abide by it. Until there was a new agreement with the government, he had to uphold the one that had been entered into. And, he could not talk with Captain Jack because the Modocs had chosen another as chief in his place.

So Captain Jack took matters into his own hands. With those who were willing to follow him, he went back to the Lost River country in California. He threatened to go on the warpath if he was not left alone, and those who attempted to reason with him were answered scornfully. He demanded that a new reservation be given to the Modocs where they had originally lived. There would be no going back to Oregon.

Winema knew that the situation was growing dangerous and that Captain Jack was determined to fight and to die if necessary. She rode many miles on horseback to his camp and begged him to return to the reservation. Once there, she said, he could better press for the new reservation. But if he did not return, he would cause trouble and there would be no hope of getting what was wanted.

But Captain Jack only turned his back on her. It was useless to talk further. She was "dead" to the people, Jack said. She had become a white woman.

Finally, a conference was held with Gen. E. R. S. Canby and Captain Jack repeated his demand for a new reservation and his refusal to return to Oregon. General Canby at last agreed, but he was overruled by a higher authority, and a detachment of cavalrymen was sent to Captain Jack's camp.

In an attempt to arrest Jack, a fight took place in which several soldiers and a large number of Indians were killed. The Modocs then fled to the lava beds on the shore of Tule Lake—an area they knew well and where it was impossible to dislodge them.

From here, the Modoc War was carried on—the last of the major Indian wars. It lasted one year. The lava beds were like a fortress and the Indians were in complete command of their situation. The lava was as hard as granite and needle sharp. No one could walk over it, and it was too difficult for even a mule. Also, it was crawling with snakes. There were caves where the people could hide and where guns could be hidden, and underground rivers provided water.

From this natural stronghold, the Indians carried on continual forays and ambushes and the soldiers were helpless to catch them. Women and children moved into the lava beds with the men, so families were complete and it seemed that they could hold out forever.

Finally, after a battle that lasted an entire day in which not one Indian was killed or wounded, a peace commission was appointed, headed by Colonel Meacham and General Canby. Winema went with the peace commission as interpreter. When the group arrived at the meeting place, she threw off her blanket and held out her hands in the sign of peace. "The whites do not want to kill you," she said. "Let us make peace." But Captain Jack refused to see her, acting as though she wasn't there. She knew that her life was in danger.

During the conference, Winema appealed to General Canby to make some sort of honest peace with her people. Three times, Captain Jack asked that the Modocs remain in their own country, and three times he was refused. As the tension mounted, Meacham, too, appealed to the general to relent and agree to the request. But Canby had promised before, and his promise had not been upheld.

Then, Captain Jack gave a sudden, quick command. He shot Canby under the right eye and his warriors ran their knives into the fallen body. As the Indians turned against Meacham, Winema threw herself against him and pleaded for his life. Still, he was shot seven times and was partially scalped when she called out that soldiers were coming and the Indians fled back to the lava beds.

Winema wrapped the barely alive Meacham in her saddle blanket and made him as comfortable as she could. Then she mounted her horse and raced to where the soldiers were waiting and brought them to the conference ground.

In the following weeks of renewed fighting, Winema nursed the terribly wounded Meacham back to health. He never forgot her selflessness, and the Indians, too, often talked among themselves of her bravery. But ties with her people were at an end.

It was not until field guns were brought into the area that the Indians were at last overcome. Captain Jack was tried and sentenced to death for his leadership of the Modoc rebellion.

In Washington, a great parade was held in Winema's

honor. James Redpath, a dramatist of that time, wrote a play about her and she acted her own role. The play was given in Independence Hall in Philadelphia and in the National Theatre in Washington as well as in many large and small cities. Winema was a special guest of President Grant in the White House, and she was honored by leading citizens wherever she appeared. Colonel Meacham wrote a book about the Modoc War and Winema. It was titled *Winema (The Woman Chief) and Her People.*

Seventeen years after the Modoc War, the government recognized Winema's services both to her own people and to the whites, by granting a pension of twenty-five dollars a month. She spent this money on the needy Indians on the reservation where she returned to live.

Winema lived to be eighty-four years old. She died in 1920 and was buried in the Modoc cemetery. Over her grave, the Daughters of the American Revolution placed a tablet reading "Wi-ne-ma—Strong Heart." A national forest has been named for this woman of the long, flowing auburn hair and the fearless spirit who carved her name on the records of the old Northwest. But these honors have come from the whites whom Winema so greatly aided. There are still Modocs who feel, like Captain Jack, that her sympathies were not with them.

E. PAULINE JOHNSON

CANADA'S FAMOUS POET

Pauline Johnson was born in 1862 in a beautiful home called Chiefswood on the Six Nations Reserve in Ontario. She was the youngest of four children and her Indian name was Tekahionwake.

The house, which is today a historic shrine, is set in deep lawns and a dark forest. It was a wedding gift for Pauline's mother, a young English woman, Emily S. Howells, who married Chief George H. M. Johnson (Onwanonsyshon), of the Mohawks. He was a member of the council of sachems, and was said to have been the greatest peacetime leader of the Six Nations Indians (originally the Five Nations).

Chiefswood was built by Chief Johnson, and combines his Indian world with the world of his white wife. One entrance faces the St. Lawrence River, in Indian fashion, and another entrance faces the road, in the white manner.

A piano, costly furniture, a well-stocked library, and fine silver and china were part of the furnishings. Among the books in the library were those written by Pauline's mother's cousin, the well-known novelist William Dean Howells.

Pauline's grandfather was John "Smoke" Johnson, a Pine Tree chief, who was an outstanding orator.

Chiefswood was the capitol of Eastern Indian Canada, and Chief Johnson was host to most of Canada's leaders as well as to important visitors to the country from other lands. Edward, Prince of Wales, who was to become King Edward VII, visited there as did Prince Arthur, the Duke of Connaught.

When the Duke came, he was little more than a child. He was to be made a chief in the Mohawk tribe and the Mohawks gathered to meet him at the station in the nearby town of Brantford.

Chief Johnson rode a jet black pony alongside the carriage of the young prince. About his shoulders, a scarlet blanket was draped. The chief and the prince enjoyed a basket of grapes together as they rode side by side to the Mohawk Chapel where the ceremony was to take place. The chapel had been built in 1785 by the great Joseph Brant and in it were a Bible and a communion set, the gifts of Queen Anne.

At the church, the prince was surrounded by 300 Mohawk braves in war paint and feathers. All carried tomahawks, scalping knives, and bows and arrows. Over and over they sounded their war whoops while the prince raised his hat. After the prince had shaken hands with each Indian, Pauline's grandfather placed his scarlet blanket on the ground and asked the prince to stand on it. When Chief Johnson was still a boy he had fought for England in the War of 1812; now following an ancient ritual he would have the honor of conferring the chieftainship on a member of England's royal family.

The chiefs of three clans received the prince into the tribe and he was given an Indian name. The ceremony ended when a deep red sash, embroidered with beads, porcupine quills, and dyed moose hair, was placed over his left shoulder and knotted at the right side.

Although other white men had received honorary titles from the Six Nations none but the duke, it is said, has had the ancient ritual with the required number of chiefs assisting. He was made the fifty-first chief in the council of sachems and his photo and that of his mother, Queen Victoria, were placed in the Six Nations council house. He later became governor-general of Canada. Pauline was a child when the ceremony took place.

Many years later, when she wrote one of her most famous books—*Flint and Feather*—she dedicated it to the Duke of Connaught as head chief of the Six Nations Indians. The red blanket on which he had stood, she used as part of her Mohawk costume when she gave poetry readings or lectures.

When Pauline was very young, she began to show a fascination for words and an intense love of poetry. Even before she could write, she composed small verses about her pets. She had a remarkable memory and could very quickly learn by heart the verses that were read to her. When she was only four, a friend of her father's asked what gift he could bring her from the city and she replied, "verses, please." Before she was twelve, she had read every line of Scott's and Longfellow's verses and much of Byron and Shakespeare.

When she was twelve, she began to write poems in earnest. She did not offer anything for publication, however, until her school days had ended. For two years she was taught at home by a nursery governess. For three years she attended an Indian day school a short distance from Chiefswood, and then she went to a central school in Brantford. She had no schooling beyond elementary school level. However, she was such an avid reader that she gained a broad general education.

The first periodical to accept Pauline's poetry was *Gems of Poetry* published in New York. As she became better known she wrote for many of the established magazines and newspapers in the United States, Canada, and London.

Her great success began when she appeared on the program for an evening of Canadian literature in Toronto. She recited her poem "A Cry from an Indian Wife," which tells the story of the Northwest Indian rebellion from the Indian point of view. This was greeted with tremendous applause, and she was the only one to be called for an encore.

The next day, Toronto papers asked why the young poet was not appearing as a professional reader. Two of the papers carried editorials asking why a volume of her poems had never been published and insisting that more should be heard of her.

An entire recital evening was then arranged. For this she wrote the poem that became her best known work— the haunting "The Song My Paddle Sings."

On this eventful evening, Pauline suffered an attack of beginner's nerves and forgot the lines of the poem. Undismayed, she quickly substituted something else and completely won the audience with her self-possession. She afterwards said she could not leave the platform in defeat and she was never defeated in time of trouble after that.

The great success of her recital led to a series of readings throughout eastern Canada. At the end of two years, she went to London and arranged with a publisher to bring out her first book, *The White Wampum*.

The doors of London's social and literary world were thrown open to her, and she was asked to give recitals in the homes of many diplomats, critics, and members of nobility. In spite of all the honors she remained a sweet, unaffected person, grateful to all who helped her, and warmly responsive to people without regard to their station in life.

The book was enthusiastically received and highly praised. Returning to Canada, Pauline made her first long trip to the Pacific coast, giving recitals at all the cities and towns along the way. From then on, she belonged to the platform world. People clamored to see and hear her and she never denied them.

She crossed the Rockies nineteen times in all and appeared in every city and town between Halifax and Vancouver. She appeared at whistle stops, in saloons and tumble down theaters, in mining camps and fishing villages. In a way, she was the modern counterpart of the wandering poet of medieval times.

Her second published book was *Canadian Born*, which sold out within a year. Although she was best known for her poems, especially the collection titled *Flint and Feather*, she also published three books of prose. One, *The Moccasin Maker*, is the story of her childhood.

Pauline made two more trips to England. On her return from the second, she toured the United States, appearing across the country as far west as Boulder, Colorado.

Although she had tremendous powers of endurance, the hardships of travel throughout northwest Canada in the early 1900s were to take their toll. Pauline settled down in Vancouver, intending to devote herself to literature, but in a short time her health completely broke down and for more than a year she was an invalid. Since she could not attend to business, a trust was formed by leading citizens of the city who collected and published, for her benefit, her later works.

When at last, as she said in one of her poems, "night shut out the day," Pauline closed her eyes. She had always had a tremendous love of life and it was not easy for her to relinquish it. But when she died in 1913 she left a rich legacy. For years her works were the best selling of any Canadian writer.

Her funeral was impressive. The cortege wound along Vancouver streets among hundreds of people from every walk of life and a huge crowd of silent, motionless Indians. She was cremated and her ashes were placed in a strongbox and buried underneath a small pool at the base of a stone memorial in Stanley Park. Two of her books were placed with the ashes. On the rocky pile there is a bronze profile plaque of Pauline Johnson, and a crossed feather and arrow and a canoe.

In 1961, she was further memorialized with the issuance of a stamp bearing her picture by the Canadian government. She is the only Indian woman to be so honored.

Pauline Johnson occupies a memorable place in Canadian literature. Although much of her writing expressed the Victorian attitudes of her time, her Indian heritage gave her a point of view and topic that struck a fresh note. The mark of her genius was that she was able to put the thoughts of one race into the literary style of another.

She was close to the white people of Canada as she was close to her own people. She often drew upon the experiences of travel for her subject matter and tried out her poems on her audiences before they were printed.

She was a truly national poet in outlook. No one at that time knew all of Canada as she did. She had driven over country where the railroad had not come, had run strange rivers, had crossed lonely lakes by canoe, and had camped where few had ever been.

In the last three verses of "The Song My Paddle Sings," one can almost see her in her beloved canoe, forging on with undaunted spirit and the brave heart

of a proud Mohawk. The poem is her monument, more
than anything else.

> Be strong, O paddle! be brave, canoe!
> The reckless waves you would plunge into.
> Reel, reel.
> On your trembling keel,
> But never a fear my craft will feel.
> We've raced the rapid, we're far ahead!
> The river slips through its silent bed.
> Sway, sway,
> As the bubbles spray
> And fall in tinkling tunes away.
> And up on the hills against the sky,
> A fir tree rocking its lullaby,
> Swings, swings,
> Its emerald wings,
> Swelling the song my paddle sings.

SUSAN LA FLESCHE PICOTTE

THE FIRST INDIAN
WOMAN PHYSICIAN

Susan La Flesche was born on the Omaha reservation in Nebraska, the sixth and youngest child in a distinguished and unusual Omaha family. The oldest child, Louis, died while still a young boy. All of the other La Flesche children made their mark in the world, and Susan was the first Indian woman physician at a time when it was rare for a white woman, even, to enter this profession.

An older sister, Susette, was the first Indian woman to crusade publicly on a national and international scale for the Indian people. She was known as Bright Eyes and she stirred the consciences and opened the purses of her audiences so that many projects were initiated for Indians. She was also a writer and a painter of skill.

Rosalie was an efficient business woman and the business head of her husband's stock feeding enterprise. She had ten children, of whom eight survived. All but one went to college and several graduated with fine records.

Marguerite was a teacher at the agency school on the reservation and often served as interpreter for congressional hearings and other meetings. Despite her frail health she was active in church and civic affairs, constantly contributing to her community.

Francis La Flesche was a notable anthropologist, who wrote many books and articles about his people. He had a law degree and spent many years in government service.

All of the La Flesche children were born in a time of transition when the tribal culture was already vanishing. Their father, Joseph (Iron Eye), was the last recognized chief of the Omahas and he is mentioned in many histories of the West that deal with Indians. He saw the rapid changes taking place and he believed that the old order was destined to vanish. He believed that it was important for the Omahas to enter the white world and he instilled in his children the principle that they must become as white people, learning to live like them, to speak, dress, act, and think like them.

Joseph La Flesche was one who had signed the treaty of 1854 by which the Omahas gave up all claim to their hunting grounds west of the Mississippi for the reservation lands bordering on the Missouri River. He had traveled widely with his French father, visiting other tribes and eastern cities. He could foresee the change that was to come, but even he was not fully prepared for the combined impact of the coming of the railroad, the slaughter of the buffalo, which was the Indians' source of food, clothing, and shelter, and the stepped-up influx of white people with an insatiable lust for land and little desire to be friendly.

Joseph La Flesche's children were born during the years between the signing of the treaty and the end of the Civil War; their growing-up years were in that critical time when too rapid change was demoralizing the Omahas and destroying their traditions. Suddenly the Omahas were subject to the control of a remote government that imposed bewildering laws that they only half-understood.

When Susette, the eldest La Flesche daughter, was born, the family lived in a traditional earth lodge. By the time Susan was born her father had helped his people build houses of log and frame, and had moved his own family into a two-story house in the agency village. The family as a whole had made a major step toward a completely new way of life and the children went on to excel in their chosen fields. They adopted many of the ways of whites, but at the same time, they spent a large part of their lives defying and openly fighting the government when harsh or unjust conditions were imposed on their people.

Susan did not learn to speak English until she went to the reservation mission and government schools. When she was fourteen, she was sent to Elizabeth, New Jersey, to the Institute for Young Ladies where two of her sisters had gone before her. Three years were spent in this school, and then Susan went to Hampton Institute in Virginia, one of the first government nonreservation schools for Indians. When she graduated, she was given a gold medal for high scholastic achievement.

There were no scholarships specifically for Indians at that time, but an organization known as the Women's National Indian Association was helping to finance professional training for Indian young people. With aid from this group, Susan was able to enter the Women's Medical College of Pennsylvania, which was located in Philadelphia. During her medical student years, Susan was often a guest in some of the most beautiful, cultured homes in the city and made many life-long friends. She graduated at the head of a class of thirty-six young women, all as earnest and dedicated as she, and she was appointed an intern at the Women's Hospital.

Susan could have continued on in private practice

when her internship was completed. But the reservation called, and the needs of her people at home were uppermost in her plan of life. She returned to Nebraska to serve as doctor at the agency school, and later as physician for the whole reservation.

This was a heavy task. The people were widely scattered over the reservation, and there were still many of the old who scoffed at the white man, and especially at his medicine. Susan often had to urge her medical help on them against their wishes.

She traveled on horseback, day or night, in all kinds of weather, caring for the thirteen hundred Omahas. There was no way to get word of illness to her quickly, if word was sent at all. Often when the news of sickness reached her, it was too late to be of any help, but she would go anyway. Perhaps she could be of some comfort. Often she had to be nurse as well as doctor, teach good hygiene and sanitation, and care for newborn babies. She had to treat all kinds of conditions entirely on her own. There was no other doctor and no hospital.

Nevertheless, she responded to every call, even through the bitter cold and deep snows of winter. No storm could hold her back and her arrival at a lonely shack or tipi might be in a state of complete exhaustion. The people most often had little food, but they would share with her a bowl of hot corn soup and a piece of venison if there had been good hunting.

Eventually, her strength could stand no more and she gave up her work temporarily to marry Henry Picotte, her sister Marguerite's husband's brother, who was part Sioux. She settled with him in the town of Bancroft and, as soon as she could, began again to practice medicine. Her patients were both Indian and white. Each night, a lamp was placed in the front window of her house so that the light would fall on the doorstep— a beacon to anyone in need of medical help.

In 1906, a year after Henry's death, the town of Walthill was founded and Susan went there to live in a comfortable, modern home. Following in the tradition of her crusading family, Susan became an outstanding community leader. She was one of the organizers of the County Medical Society, health officer for the town, and a member of the State Medical Society. She was on the board of the State Federation of Women's Clubs and lobbied at the state legislature for better public health laws.

She also went to Washington to make certain that no liquor would ever be sold in the reservation town, and she established a hospital in Walthill.

Traditionally, the Omahas had never had a woman leader, but now they listened to Susan and looked to her for guidance. It was said that in her twenty-five years of medical practice, she had treated every member of the tribe and saved the lives of many.

She was the only Indian ever appointed medical missionary by the Presbyterian Board of Home Missions but she did not restrict her activities to medicine alone. She tried in every way to advance her people economically, socially, and spiritually.

When the reservation was established, Omaha lands were held in trust for the tribe and their property was administered for them by the government. The people themselves had no control over what was done and nothing to say about it. Under this system, they were growing restive, resentful, and decidedly rebellious. When it was suggested that this trust arrangement be extended for ten years beyond the stipulated period of the treaty, Susan, like her sister, Susette, became an articulate voice for the tribe. She appeared before the secretary of the interior to protest this extension.

In the name of justice and humanity, she asked for a

more liberal interpretation of the law pertaining to the Omahas. She said that she would willingly and gladly cooperate with anything for the good of the tribe, but would fight "good and hard against anything that was to their detriment," as she believed this to be.

A law was finally passed granting the Omahas individual ownership of land within the boundaries of the reservation.

For a number of years, Susan suffered from an infection of the facial bones, which caused her extreme suffering, but which did not lessen her humanitarian activities. Even though she lived far differently from those of her people who clung to tribal values she was never out of touch with them. She was one of them by blood and understanding, surely; she was one of them who had gone ahead on the trail.

Presbyterian clergymen officiated at her funeral services when she died, but the closing prayer was given by an aged Omaha Indian in the tribal language. She would have appreciated this.

Physicians among Indian woman are few, but there is one especially deserving of mention. This is Dr. L. Rosa Minoka Hill, a Mohawk, who was born on the St. Regis reservation in New York.

Rosa Minoka was orphaned as a child and was brought up by Quakers. She graduated from Grahame Institute in Philadelphia and, like Susan La Flesche, entered the Women's Medical College of Pennsylvania. Other medical colleges did not readily accept women as students, and most of them not at all.

After completing her internship, Dr. Minoka practiced in Philadelphia for five years. Then she married Charles A. Hill, an Oneida, and moved with him to his reservation in Wisconsin.

Her husband did not wish her to practice medicine so

she did not, but she ministered to many of the poor without pay. Ten years later, she was a widow with six children, the youngest only five months old.

She had a very small income from a trust estate, and the farm produced a little also. With that, she kept up what charity practice she could. Actually, this amounted to a large practice. Often, she would drive the eleven miles into the town of Green Bay to get medicine for a sufferer for which she might never be paid. Even if the roads were icy and the snow was deep, she would hitch up her team and make the journey.

When the depression of the 1930s wiped out Dr. Hill's trust fund, she could no longer provide her family with even the necessities of life. So, thirty-five years after her graduation from medical college, Dr. Hill appeared before the state board of medical examiners to secure a Wisconsin license. She borrowed the money for her physician's license and for a basic science license and began active practice. Still, no Indian in need was ever turned away, and on the reservation there were many such Indians.

She was forced to retire from overwork during World War II and in 1947 she was awarded the Indian Achievement Award.

Dr. Lucille Johnson Marsh, a Tuscarora, was another early Indian woman physician. Dr. Marsh was the daughter of a physician—Dr. Philip T. Johnson, a chief of the tribe, who practiced in Erie, Pennsylvania, for many years.

Dr. Marsh obtained her medical degree at Ohio State University. She was a pediatrician and for a number of years was director of the Infant Welfare Clinic of the city of Miami. She was chief of the Children's Bureau, Department of Maternal and Child Health, Division of Indian Health, U. S. Public Health Service at the time of her death.

Matoaks als Rebecka daughter to the mighty Prince
Powhatan Emperour of Attanoughkomouck als Virginia
converted and baptized in the Christian faith, and
Wife to the Wor:ll Mr Tho: Rolff.

Pocahontas. From a portrait made
in London c. 1616 by an unknown
artist. (*Smithsonian Institution
National Anthropological Archives*)

Sarah Winnemucca
(*Nevada State Museum*)

Sacajawea. Statue on
the grounds of the North
Dakota State capital. (*State
Historical Society of North
Dakota*)

Winema
(*Oregon Historical Society*)

Pauline Johnson
(*Public Archives of Canada*)

BELOW Susan La Flesche
Picotte (*Nebraska State
Historical Society*)

RIGHT Gertrude Simmons
Bonnin

Roberta Campbell Lawson

Pablita Velarde

Maria and Julian Martinez

LEFT Annie Dodge Wauneka

ABOVE Esther Burnett Horne

Marjorie Tallchief

Maria Tallchief

Wilma Victor

Elaine Abraham Ramos

GERTRUDE SIMMONS BONNIN

A MODERN PROGRESSIVE

Gertrude Bonnin was known among her people, the Yankton Sioux, as Zitkala-sha, or Red Bird. She was born in 1875 on the Yankton Sioux reservation and was raised as an Indian child in a traditional family. Most of her childhood was spent in a wind-blown tipi close to the Missouri River. Among Indians, children are loved and raised with tenderness. But they are not permitted to vie for attention or to be bold in the presence of adults. Gertrude was taught no fear except that of imposing herself upon others.

When she was twelve years old, she was sent to a Quaker missionary school for Indians in Wabash, Indiana. Her brother, three years older than herself, had gone there. Gertrude was lured to the school by tales told by the recruiting missionaries of a ride on an iron horse, of the beautiful countryside, and of trees that grew big, red apples—hers for the picking.

Gertrude's mother was unwilling to let her go, but the child's eagerness wore down her resistance. She decided, too, that Gertrude should be an educated woman for there would be many more "palefaces" in the country as time went on and increasing problems for those who would try to live in traditional Indian fashion.

At the school, Gertrude was not especially happy. She ran away and hid in fear when told that her long braids would be cut off. She understood little of what was said to her, but as her understanding grew, the sensitive child keenly felt the comments about Indians that reflected on her people and background.

When she returned to the reservation at the end of her three-year term, she was torn between the beliefs of her people and the new ones that she had been taught. Her mother wrapped herself in aloofness because there was a deep chasm between them. Gertrude's existence was a joyless one. She was neither completely Indian nor completely white. She was Indian in features and coloring, but she no longer thought as one. It was difficult for her to recall her first language, and she could express her thoughts only in a limited way, not with the richness of Sioux imagery and phrasing. So mother and daughter spoke almost as strangers in a stilted fashion that could not convey any feelings of deep emotion.

Yet many of the white attitudes Gertrude expressed had been thrust upon her and were basically alien to her.

Finally, after four years of reservation living, this time in a log house, she came to the conclusion that the Indian had to find his way in the white man's world if he was to survive. She could no longer bear the misery of her circumstances and decided to reenter school.

Gertrude graduated from school at nineteen and with her diploma in her hand again went against her mother's desire that she return home. She entered Earlham College for two years, studying to be a teacher. But she made no friends. She stored up in her mind every little remark that seemed to carry a slight, and she kept those who would be friendly at arm's length, spending most of her time alone in her room.

When an oratorical contest was announced, she decided to enter, driven by a need to prove herself. As she listened to the speeches of the others, she was consumed with a longing to win—and win, she did. The first place award went to her.

Her classmates gave her a bouquet of lovely roses, and though she was touched by this, she still discouraged their friendliness and went to her room when the contest was over, alone and lonely.

A second contest was held at the state capital, and Gertrude was entered in that, also. As she waited her turn, some of the students in the audience held up a white flag with the figure of an Indian girl drawn on it and labeled squaw. There were also shouted slurs. Gertrude sat with stony face and set teeth, pretending that she did not notice. But the hurt rankled. When one of the two prizes was given to her, the flag was hauled down and there were no more unkind remarks.

In her room that night, she sat gazing into the fireplace. She laughed, more in bitterness than in triumph, and even though she had won a victory, there was still a pain in her heart.

After college, Gertrude became a teacher of Indian students at the famous Carlisle Indian School in Pennsylvania. Carlisle had been founded by an army man, Col. Richard H. Pratt. He believed that assimilation was the only way for Indians, and all of his students were taught trades and sent out into white communities to practice them. There was nothing soft or sentimental about the colonel. He would create opportunities for Indians and it was up to them to take advantage of them. Carlisle produced some outstanding Indian individuals, and nearly all of the students made good under the "sink or swim" policies.

The children and young people came to Carlisle right from the reservations or from army prison camps. Their hair was long and they were dressed in native clothing. Gertrude's heart ached for them. She saw herself as a child, and well understood the fright and sorrow they would experience. But gradually, they were transformed as she herself had been.

By now, she had developed a love of music and an ability to play. She enrolled at the Boston Conservatory of Music and in 1900 traveled to Paris with the Carlisle Indian school band as violin soloist. The band played at the Paris Exposition.

Gertrude was also a talented writer, and she wrote several charming autobiographical essays. These were published in the *Atlantic Monthly*. She also wrote some Indian legends for *Harper's Monthly* and later a collection of Indian legends that were published in book form. The illustrations were drawn by another noted Indian woman—Angel DeCora, a Winnebago, who was an art teacher at Carlisle.

Once more, Gertrude returned to her Sioux country where she was employed as a clerk on the Standing Rock reservation. The government wanted to make use of educated Indians among their own people in order to set examples. There she met and married Raymond Bonnin, also a Sioux and an agency employee.

The young couple were sent to the Ute reservation in Utah and remained there for fourteen years. Gertrude was now and again employed as a clerk and briefly as a teacher. She organized a band for the children, remembering the one at Carlisle. She was also a home demonstration teacher, showing the Indian women how to cook with white man's foods, how to keep house in the white man's fashion, and how to care for children as the white man did. She had a boy child of her own.

While living among the Utes, Mrs. Bonnin was in

touch with a newly formed organization, the Society of American Indians. This led to her life work in Indian reform and as a spokeswoman for her people.

The society had been founded by six well-educated Indians and was the first organization to be managed exclusively by Indians. Membership was restricted to Indians. The goals included not only government reforms, but the codification of laws relating to Indians, the employment of Indians by the Bureau of Indian Affairs, the opening of the Court of Claims to all equitable claims of Indian tribes pertaining to land settlements, and to the preservation of the true history of the race.

In time, the program advocated by the society was one of assimilation, citizenship for all Indians, the abolishment of the Bureau of Indian Affairs, and the termination of all property held in common.

Some of these goals were achieved in total or in part, but many Indians have not been too accepting of assimilation and the abolishment of government services and reservations. Among Indians, these are highly controversial subjects.

Mrs. Bonnin was elected secretary of the society in 1916. She and her husband then made Washington their home. As the official representative of the society, she lectured from coast to coast on Indian affairs and she edited the society's publication, *The American Indian Magazine.*

The society lasted only four years. Six years later, Mrs. Bonnin formed the National Council of American Indians and was its president until her death in 1938. She was most energetic in lobbying for Indian legislation in Washington.

Perhaps one of her greatest contributions to the cause of her people was her influence in securing the active interest of the General Federation of Women's Clubs, with its thousands of members, in Indian affairs. She pursuaded the federation to establish an Indian Welfare committee and to work intensively in behalf of Indian rights.

Together with the Indian Rights Association—at that time the leading national Indian-interest organization—the federation sponsored an investigation into the treatment of the various tribes by the government. Mrs. Bonnin conducted this investigation and also directed the federation's interest in working for the enfranchisement of Indians as well as for improvements in education, health centers, hospitals, the conservation of resources, and the preservation of Indian culture.

The appointment of an expert commission headed by the late Lewis Meriam of the Institute for Governmental Research surveyed conditions among Indians. The resulting report led President Hoover to appoint two leading members of the Indian Rights Association as commissioner and assistant commissioner of the Bureau of Indian Affairs.

An earlier accomplishment was the passage in 1924 of the Indian Citizenship Bill, introduced by Charles Curtis, himself a Kaw Indian and a long-time Congressman and whip of the Senate. He was to become vice-president of the United States under Herbert Hoover.

Mrs. Bonnin was one who went among Indian people urging them to press for the bill and to accept the vote. Many Indians were suspicious of this move. They were fearful that this meant taxing their trust lands and perhaps the loss of lands and property, and they had to be convinced of the advantages, to them, of voting.

The groundwork was laid for many reforms in the BIA, but in spite of all good intentions little action took place. For one reason, there was a severe drought and economic depression. The Indian Bureau could not cope with the acute problems they caused any more than any other government agency could. Mrs. Bonnin, however, turned away from the Republican administration and advised Indians to use their recently acquired voting privilege to put Franklin Roosevelt in office.

Both Captain and Mrs. Bonnin continued to work for the National Council of American Indians and to lobby in behalf of Indians, particularly the Sioux and the Utes. Mrs. Bonnin still lectured extensively, appearing in a beautiful Sioux buckskin costume, to dramatize her Indian identity. She wrote less and less, but revived her interest in music and composed an Indian opera called *Sun Dance.*

Gertrude Bonnin died in Washington at the age of sixty-one. She was buried in Arlington Cemetery. As an Indian "progressive"—a white-educated Indian who pressed for reforms both on and off the reservation—she was in the vanguard of those who championed their people. Her career was a combination of the achievements and frustrations that are the lot of those Indians who work in behalf of their people.

ROBERTA CAMPBELL LAWSON

LEADER OF
THREE MILLION WOMEN

Roberta Campbell Lawson, as president of the General Federation of Women's Clubs, headed the largest organization of women in the world. She was in office from 1935 to 1938, coming to that position over an unusual and historic trail.

She was born at Alluwe, Indian Territory, in 1878, of Indian and Scotch descent. Six miles downriver from her home was the adjoining ranch where another famous Indian was born. This was Will Rogers, the nationally beloved Cherokee humorist. Indian Territory, which was later to become part of Oklahoma, was open country at that time.

Roberta's father was J. E. Campbell of a pioneer Virginia family. He came to the territory and built up a prosperous mercantile and cattle business. Her mother was Emeline Journeycake, the daughter of the Rev. Charles Journeycake, the last chief of the Delawares and a very great man.

Charles was the son of a remarkable woman, Sally Journeycake, a Wyandotte married into the Delaware tribe. Sally was a devout Christian. Strangely enough, she was influenced to become one by a homeless black man who was taken in by her father. The black man sang hymns that appealed to Sally. When the Methodists started a mission among her people, she became their interpreter and before long became a Christian convert.

The Delawares, on the other hand, had been Christian converts. They were cruelly massacred at the hands of the whites, and those remaining were driven from their homes. Embittered by what had taken place, they refused to have any more to do with Christian missionaries.

In order to escape further persecution, the Delawares decided to move to Kansas. The journey west over rough wilderness trails took two years. Throughout, Sally was the only one to sing the praises of the Lord. Every night while the Indians danced around their drums, she gathered her children together and taught them about Jesus. Sally's behavior made a deep impression upon the Delawares. When they settled in Kansas, for the first time in forty-six years they allowed missionaries to come among them.

Charles was ten when his mother was converted. He was the first Delaware converted and baptized west of the Mississippi and the first Protestant baptized in what is now Kansas. He began to preach soon after his conversion but he was not ordained as a minister until he was fifty-two.

He was chosen chief of the tribe when he was forty-four, but the government did not recognize him as such until the Delawares removed to Indian Territory. Under his leadership, the tribe adopted a written constitution, which contained well-defined laws for the protection of the freedom and rights of the people. He also helped to establish Bacone College in Oklahoma, which for many years, was the only college for Indians in the country.

On the cornerstone of the beautiful chapel on the campus are inscribed the words of Charles Journeycake: They are:

> We have been broken up and moved six times. We have been despoiled of our property. We thought when we moved across the Missouri River and had paid for our homes in Kansas we were safe, but in a few years the white man wanted our country. We had good farms, built comfortable houses, and big barns. We had schools for our children and churches where we listened to the same gospel the white man listened to. The white man came into our country from Missouri and drove our cattle and our horses away and if our people followed them, they were killed. We try to forget these things, but we would not forget that the white man brought to us the blessed gospel of Christ, the Christian's hope. This more than pays for all we have suffered.

Roberta was devoted to her Indian grandfather. From him, she learned the legends and chants of his people. He taught her to love the sounds and scents of nature and the power of faith and loyalty. From him, too, came her own fine qualities of leadership.

From her grandfather's sermons, she gained a deep spiritual reverence. To her, his words were wonderful and she wanted everyone to hear them. Once she slapped a little girl in church because she wasn't paying attention.

Another time, she gave away a pair of newly purchased shoes to a poor woman who had none, so that she could come to church.

Roberta's home was a comfortable one. There was a schoolhouse on the grounds where she was taught by a private tutor. There were ponies and bicycles for her and her brother to ride and a tennis court. The house was nicely furnished with many good paintings and books, a piano and other musical instruments. It was al-

ways overflowing with guests, both expected and un-
expected. All were graciously entertained.

At Hardin College, Roberta was a serious music student. She learned to play the piano well and could sing
beautifully. She could also compose. To her, music was
a lifelong delight. She wrote a number of Indian songs
and translated a number of Indian chants. She also tran-
scribed old Delaware melodies that would have been lost.
She wrote a book on Indian music and gathered together one of the most valuable collections of Indian
musical instruments and materials in the country.

When she returned from college, she formed a club of
four members. The purpose was to promote friendship
and culture. The group rode about the countryside on
horseback, telling people of their aims.

When she was twenty-three, Roberta married Eugene
B. Lawson who had come to the territory from Kentucky to practice law. The young couple made their
home in Nowata. This community, with the approaching
conversion of Indian Territory to statehood, was rapidly
developing. The Lawsons were leaders in its civic and
financial progress.

It was then that Roberta's keen interest in women's
affairs began to strengthen. She helped to organize and
was president of the town's first women's club which
was also the first federated club in the territory. She
helped to establish a park and the public library. She
was also active in the YWCA. Her only child was a boy,
but this did not divert her active participation in projects related to girls and women.

She became increasingly involved in larger responsibilities, especially in club work, and served as president
of the Oklahoma Federation of Women's Clubs. With a
comfortable fortune from Mr. Lawson's expanding oil
interests, the Lawsons now moved to Tulsa. Roberta
served as a director of the Oklahoma Historical Society

and was the only woman trustee for the University of Tulsa. She was a thirteen-year member of the Board of Regents of the College for Women at Chickasaw.

Will Rogers, now at the peak of his fame, asked her to become executive chairman of a committee to administer a huge fund that he had collected through benefit appearances for drought relief in states hard hit by an unprecedented dry spell—especially Oklahoma.

In 1933, Roberta was a member of the General Federation of Women's Clubs World Friendship Tour. While in Czechoslovakia she presented several programs on Indian music, appearing in a beaded buckskin Indian costume.

She was second and first vice president of the federation before her election to the presidency. For her three-year administration, she chose the theme Education for Living. She was particularly involved in the establishment of a national Academy of Public Service, comparable to West Point and Annapolis, which was to prepare students for government posts. Indians, too, were not neglected. She never lost sight of her Indian people and their need for help. She was ever the champion of their cause, speaking out in their behalf and interesting others in working for them.

When Roberta Lawson moved to Tulsa, she began her collection of Indian artifacts from the time of the Mound Builders up to contemporary hand work. She also established a library on Indian history including rare and out of print books.

A tall, regal, very erect woman with a warm manner and much charm, Roberta Lawson had wide, dark eyes and an Indian contour to her face. She wore her jet black hair piled on her head in coronet braids.

Her incentive was faith, her secret of progress a steady purpose, her goal service to others, and her reward a love of life. This philosophy came mainly from

Charles Journeycake, who taught her that through hearthstone friendships people come to understand one another. She often said that women must link the hearthstones of the world together.

Roberta Lawson died in 1940 two years after serving her term as president of the General Federation of Women's Clubs. After her death, her collection of Indian artifacts and books on Indian history was placed on display in the Philbrook Art Center in Tulsa, the city on which she left an indelible imprint.

PABLITA VELARDE

ARTIST OF THE PUEBLOS

Pablita Velarde is considered the principal painter of
Pueblo Indian life and one of the country's great artists.
She has reached a high point in the visual interpretation
of her people and is an inspiration to other Indian artists. She knows and honors the best of Pueblo culture
and strives to communicate this knowledge and appre-
ciation to others.

Pablita was born in the fall of the year 1918 in the
pueblo of Santa Clara. Her father's mother, Qualupita,
a medicine woman, helped with the ritual of birth and of
naming. The child had no name at all until four days
after her birth because the Indians believed that the
spirit of the baby did not arrive until then. At the proper
time she was given the name Tse Tsan, meaning golden
dawn, because she was born at daybreak.

Grandmother Qualupita placed hot coals and two pine
boughs in a pottery bowl which was offered in six direc-
tions with a prayer that the child's life would warm and
brighten others. Then the baby was held up and named
Tse Tsan as sacred corn meal was sprinkled at the door-

way of the home. All those who came to the naming ceremony also gave a name to the child, but these were usually forgotten.

When she was named, Pablita, as she was later called, was wrapped in soft skins and placed in a cradleboard. This was hung from the roof beams of the room or carried on her mother's back.

The house had two rooms—the living room in which the family slept and the kitchen, where they ate. The kitchen had a fireplace with a chimney, but the cooking was done outdoors. The staple foods were corn meal mush, fried bread, a bread that was baked in the outside oven, hot chili, fresh or dried deer meat cooked with corn, rabbits, turkeys, beans, wild vegetables, and edible weeds.

Pablita was only three when her mother died, leaving two older sisters and a new baby. Pablita and the baby were stricken with an illness that took away their sight. Their father, who knew something about Indian medicines, treated the children, and in two years Pablita's sight returned, though her eyes remained weak.

The Velarde family lived at the edge of the pueblo. When the great ceremonial dances were held, the children watched from the plaza. Pablita was deeply impressed with the colorful and imaginative costumes. The kachina dancers, who wore strange masks representing various spirits, frightened her. But she absorbed every detail of all the dances, her mind photographing them as if it were a camera.

Once a month, the children attended mass in the ancient church at the pueblo, which went back to the coming of the Spaniards. They always went at Christmas and Easter and on St. Claire's feast day in August.

Pablita's father sent his children to a nearby day school. When Pablita was six, she and her sisters were sent to a large mission school in Santa Fe. Pablita, who spoke only a little English, was placed in kindergarten.

The children did not go home for vacations, but their father came to see them twice a year. He gave each one fifty cents, which seemed like a lot of money. Later, they came home in the summer time. Pablita worked on the farm, let the cattle out in the morning and put them back in their pen at night, and rode horseback.

When the father moved up into the mountains, Pablita rode down the mountainside to get water for the animals and for drinking and cooking.

Sometimes Pablita went to live with her grandmother in the pueblo. From her, she learned many customs and skills. Grandmother roasted gypsum rocks and crushed them into powder. When whitewash was added, this mixture was used to paint the house walls. Painted designs bordered the windows and the fireplaces were decorated with mountain, cloud, and rain symbols.

Grandmother was a good pottery maker and she taught Pablita this art, also. Pablita liked the feel of the clay under her hands. She liked the shaping of it, smoothing out the kinks and rough spots and forming a graceful vessel.

On the Santa Clara reservation there are famous ruins called Puye, or Pueblo of the Clouds, where the main cliff dwelling included two thousand rooms. Ancestors of the Santa Clara people had once lived there and Pablita found the ruins a fascinating place to play. Here and there she discovered flat rocks with pictures on them. She tried to imagine what the pictures were and made up stories about what she thought they said. When she had been blind, she had formed the habit of storing up mental pictures. Now she stored in memory those rock pictures.

In the summer months, when the work of the farm was done, the father told his children stories from the past. They were mostly religious stories. A few were creation stories of the time when the Pueblos first came upon the earth, led from an underground world by Spider Woman.

The images that the stories brought out remained in Pablita's mind. As she listened, the pictures would come as if they were painted before her eyes.

When she finished her studies at the mission school, Pablita transferred to the Santa Fe government school. Here she met Dorothy Dunn, a teacher who was pioneering in the revival of Indian art. Miss Dunn taught Pablita to paint and encouraged her in learning tribal symbols.

In company with other Indian artists, she took part in the creation of a style of painting unlike any other. It was born of a cultural tradition, unchanged but built upon. Many famous Indian painters were students of Dorothy Dunn who established the first Indian art school in the United States.

Pablita learned the basic facts of colors, how to handle brushes, and how to express action from memory. She experimented with old methods of grinding raw clays and rocks.

One of her first paintings was of a group of women of Santa Clara molding clay into the large jars called ollas. She began by making a sketch in charcoal and then filling in with colored chalk. When it satisfied her, she made a final pencil sketch on watercolor paper and laid in opaque color flat with almost no outlining. The painting was a simple one, but it was true to life, and viewers were drawn by its honesty of expression. The Santa Clara women were a favorite subject. She painted scenes of women in various activities. All had the same honest strength.

Then, as her inner talent caught fire, her mind filled with other ideas. She turned to the ceremonials of her people, remembering them with photographic detail.

One famous painting is a scene of the plaza at the pueblo while a ceremonial is taking place. Spectators watch from the roof tops, and the dancers perform with perfectly detailed steps and hand gestures. The painting is alive with action, as if a movement were suddenly suspended and would as suddenly continue again. One expects this to happen with the painting style of Pablita's.

The more she painted, the more Pablita became separated from her people. She thought differently than they, for she thought with the insight and understanding of an artist. Her art was not for Indians; it was to tell about Indians.

Neither did she think as a non-Indian. Her upbringing had conditioned her to certain traditional Indian viewpoints. She was adrift on a sea that lay between two lands—that of the pueblo and that of white America.

At the end of her first year in the government school, when she had barely finished eighth grade, Pablita entered a number of her paintings of Santa Clara women in a school exhibit. They attracted the attention of Olive Rush who was preparing a series of murals for the Chicago Century of Progress exposition. She selected one of Pablita's paintings for exhibit in the New Mexico building at the exposition. Through Miss Rush, Pablita found new avenues open to her. She was signed to do a mural in oils of Pueblo life in Santa Clara for a federal art project. As she became a better artist, she was able to make use of a wider range of materials.

All this shocked the conservative people of her home. Painting was a task reserved for the men and Pablita was looked upon as something of a rebel.

Her father had remarried and had a new family and Pablita no longer went to his home. A relationship that had been close was close no longer. When she returned to Santa Clara, she lived with an older sister.

Her father, though, tried to influence her to give up

painting and learn to type. It would be better for her than art, he felt—a more appropriate activity for a woman. So Pablita came home and entered the high school of a nearby town for a business course. She had lived in boarding schools for ten years and it was strange to go to a public school. She attended for a little more than a year and then went back to the government school in Santa Fe. She graduated from there, the first of her family with a high school diploma.

This, too, did not go unnoticed by the people of her pueblo. She was again looked upon as different. At that time the girls of Santa Clara seldom completed high school, and most did not even go beyond elementary school.

For a while, Pablita was an assistant teacher at the pueblo day school. Then she was invited by Ernest Thompson Seton to go along with him and his wife on a cross-country lecture trip. She would care for the Seton baby and perhaps demonstrate pottery making. On this trip, she met many people, gaining new poise and a broader knowledge of life.

Returning to Santa Fe, she was asked to work on a mural for an Indian store in Albuquerque. Then she was asked to do a mural for Bandelier National Monument Museum in Frijoles Canyon. This was a cliff dwelling that was inhabited centuries ago. The remains of the houses still stand. The people were farmers who planted their fields in the valley and carried their food and water up the steep walls of the cliff by ladders which were pulled up when danger threatened.

This was one of Pablita's happiest assignments. She painted the ways of life of these ancient people, the work taking nearly a year. Then she returned to Santa Clara to build her own house. House building has been done by the Pueblo woman for as long as anyone knows. It is considered a woman's art. Pablita's house had three rooms, with walls of plastered adobe. Inside, she white-washed the walls as her grandmother had taught her. Her first furniture was a bed, a table, and a set of dishes. She used her home for an art studio as well as for living.

To earn money, she made Indian drums for a trader's shop, but this paid very little. She made small paintings which she displayed in Santa Fe on weekends, and she did well with them.

Then, she took employment as a switchboard operator for the Bureau of Indian Affairs in Albuquerque. She was most unhappy in this job because it offered no outlet for her artistic ability. She met a young man, Herbert Hardin, who was a night watchman for the Bureau, and when Pablita was twenty-three, they were married.

Pablita preferred to live off the reservation, so the Hardins made their home in Albuquerque. She did not think that Indians should remain in close-knit communities, entirely to themselves. She wanted to win acceptance as a person and for herself, not because there was a sentimental value attached to her being an Indian.

In her marriage, Pablita again went against Pueblo custom. Santa Clara girls could choose their husbands, but seldom did they marry out of the tribe, and almost never a non-Indian.

Pablita continued to work until her husband was drafted for military service and left for basic training in Texas. Expecting her first child, she followed him. With decent housing impossible to find, she returned to Albuquerque to live with Herbert's relatives. When her daughter, Helen, was born, she took the baby to Santa Clara for the naming ritual.

Pablita's grandmother took charge of the ceremony as she had done for Pablita herself. Helen was named Blue Corn Tassel, but among the other names given to her was that of Little Standing Spruce, given by Pablita's father. It was the name of his first wife, Pablita's mother, and is the name that Helen continued to use throughout her own outstanding art career.

Now mother and daughter joined Herbert in Pennsylvania for four very hard years. When he was ordered to California, Pablita went home once more to await the birth of her second child, Herbert, Jr. She remained at Santa Clara with her children, waiting for the war to end and for Herbert to return. She made jewelry, painted, and created small dolls.

At last the family was reunited. Herbert enrolled in the University of California to pursue studies in police work under the G.I. bill. But Pablita had difficulty breathing in the California climate. She was forced to return with the children to Santa Clara. What money there was had to be used for Herbert's schooling. So Pablita went back to Bandelier to paint again. The paintings of this period are among her finest and of great value to those who study the sciences of man.

When Herbert received his degree in criminology, he joined the Albuquerque police force. Now the Hardins had a pleasant home on a pretty street.

Pablita continued to grow as a painter and to gain fame. She won many prizes in competitions and has won many since. Her first and most important award was the Grand Prize in the Philbrook Art Center exhibition in Tulsa in 1948. She became increasingly famous for her earth paintings. For these, she collected clays and stones and ground them by hand on an Indian grinding stone. The powder was sifted into jars and mixed with glue and water.

These and other methods used by Pablita required equipment and space. She put her kitchen into service for painting and for making frames for her completed pictures. She also made Indian dolls, purses, and other articles, entered art shows, and spoke about her work.

Unfortunately, Herbert found all of this irritating.

The clutter in the house annoyed him and he resented Pablita's constant business. At first, he was proud of her success and grateful for the help she had given him. Now, he did not like the amount of time she gave to her art and the widespread attention she was receiving. There was a widening gulf between them.

In 1954, with twelve other Indian artists and artisans, Pablita was decorated with the *Ordre des Palmes Académiques* by the French government. It was the first time that any Indian artists had been recognized by a foreign government.

When Pablita was commissioned to paint a large mural for a restaurant in Houston, the work left her physically and mentally exhausted. She felt a need to restore herself by returning to Santa Clara and renewing ties with her father. He was now an old man in his seventies, and Pablita sat with him by the hour under the shade of a great cottonwood tree. There were long silences between them. Each had to find the way back over lost years.

Remembering the stories her father had told when she was a child, Pablita spoke of writing and illustrating them. At first the old man would not listen. But she kept pointing out that there would be no one to carry on the tradition when he was gone. The stories would be lost to the people forever. Finally her father agreed. By sharing his stories together, the two once more found a closeness of spirit that is now a cherished memory.

Pablita made a painting of her father which is considered her finest work. It shows an old man telling stories to a group of children surrounding him. Their faces are rapt and their bodies bent close with attention. The milky way and the constellations are part of a background of tremendous distance and against this the ancestors, migrating from another world, are marching. There are Pueblo symbols and designs of birds, animals, and a spider. An extended village is woven into the background. Because of Pablita's skillful handling of colors, the painting is infused with a mystical light that is awe-inspiring.

Old Father won the Grand Prize in the 1955 Intertribal Ceremonials exhibit at Gallup, New Mexico. In that show, Pablita also won all top honors and firsts in three categories.

Herbert, by now, had departed, completely frustrated with the dedication to art that permeated his home. Pablita continued to work. She found a publisher for the collection of her father's stories, each beautifully illustrated with her own drawings. The book, published in 1960, was acclaimed as one of the best books of the year. It aroused so much interest among younger Indians that some began to try to illustrate their own tribal legends.

The first few years after her divorce were extremely difficult for Pablita. Because of her religion, she could not look forward to a new marriage, but she had to build a new life. She painted constantly, creating a wide range of earth paintings of scenes, abstract compositions, and ceremonies. She gave many talks, appearing in Pueblo dress. She entered the major art shows. Each painting had a special meaning related to an Indian past.

In 1968, she received the Philbrook special trophy for outstanding contributions to Indian art—so far, the only woman to have this recognition. One of her paintings was presented by President Johnson to the Prime Minister of Denmark.

Her success has not come without paying a high price —that of hard and endless work.

Now and again she returned to Santa Clara, but it was no longer the familiar home of her childhood. The old two-story adobe houses were falling down and were replaced with modern homes. Each house had a TV set. The people seldom spoke their own language, if they still could, and they knew even less about the old ceremonies and religious beliefs. The legends were never heard. That which Pablita had said to her father had come to pass— the legends were no longer told for there was no one to tell them. A pattern of life had merged into the past.

Pablita bought one of the modern houses. Using a tape recorder, she began to talk with the older people, hoping to preserve what remained in their minds of old traditions and customs. She spent many hours explaining what she was doing and why to the tribal council. But, after some months of work, she began to sense an unseen, hostile force directed against herself and she abandoned this project. All of the material was placed in safekeeping and she returned to Albuquerque, which is her home today.

The Santa Clara Indians point to Pablita with pride, for she is the most famous and the greatest artist among Indian women. Her name is known around the world. They speak of her as one does of those who have gone far beyond to stand on a mountain top—and Pablita Velarde does stand on a mountain top in a golden dawn.

MARIA MONTOYA MARTINEZ

MASTER ARTISAN

Maria Martinez has lived all her life except for brief absences in the Pueblo where she was born. Her family were "traditionalists." That is, they remained true to the old ways and customs. San Ildefonso is a small Pueblo, but through Maria it became one of the most famous. The Spaniards first visited the Pueblo about five hundred years ago, in 1593, but it is much older than that.

Maria's father, Tomas, was a farmer. Her mother, Reyes, took care of the house and raised their three daughters. The oldest sister helped her father in the fields.

Maria and her younger sister were close companions. They built for themselves a small house, adding to it each year and caring for it completely. In this way they learned the skill of house construction. This was always done by the Pueblo women, who, unlike the women of most other tribes had not customarily carried on the work of planting and caring for the crops. Farm work was done by the men—probably because in ancient times, the people lived in cliff houses that were often a

105

long way from the fields and the men were better able
to travel the distances between them.

In their house, Maria and her sister each had her own
grinding stone for corn, her own room, and her own
fireplace. They learned to be good housekeepers.

Maria's aunt taught them how to make pottery. Maria
liked to work with the soft clay and shape it with her
hands into bowls. At first her work was lopsided, but
her aunt never criticized her. She only pointed out how
she could improve her work and gradually Maria made
better and better bowls.

When Maria contracted smallpox, it was thought she
would not live. Her mother nursed her constantly, and
promised the Lord that Maria would be sent on a pilgrimage if she recovered. The Montoya family followed
their traditional beliefs, but like others of the Pueblo,
they were also Catholics. When the Spaniards had come
into New Mexico, they had gained many converts. An old
Spanish church still stood at San Ildefonso. It was not
unusual for Reyes to make such a vow. Maria had been
baptized and confirmed in the church.

Maria did get well, and as soon as she was able, she
walked with her father more than ten miles to the Sanctuary of the Holy Child in the village of Chimayo. There,
she was taken into a small room near the altar. There
was a deep hole in the floor of this room, and after re-
moving her clothes, Maria climbed down into it and
rubbed herself with dirt. The Indians believed that this
dirt was sacred and had great healing power. She
brought out a small bottle filled with the dirt when she
left. This was mixed with water and she drank it every
day for four days.

Reyes and the other children accompanied Maria on
her pilgrimage to the sanctuary. Everything was done as
a family. No one in the family acted for individual gain,
and no one in the Pueblo tried to get ahead of any other

person. The unity of the family and of the people had to be preserved, for this was the ancient teaching.

Throughout the year, there were many Indian ceremonials at San Ildefonso and Maria took part in all of them. She also went to day school until she was sent to Santa Fe with her sister to attend St. Catherine's mission school. The two girls were chosen by the governor of the Pueblo to go to this school (and this was considered an honor).

The sisters remained at school for two years. Then their schooling ended, for it was not considered proper for a Pueblo girl to have any more. When Maria returned home, however, she helped with the housekeeping at the day school that she had once attended.

A young man of the Pueblo named Julian Martinez also helped around the school, doing chores and odd jobs. Although he lived at San Ildefonso, Maria did not know him. His father was a saddlemaker.

At the Pueblo, farming was the most important occupation and most of the young men farmed. Because Julian did not farm, the villagers looked upon him as someone who was not quite respectable.

Since they both worked at the school, Maria saw a lot of Julian, and she came to love him. She understood the restless nature that made him different. He hated farming and it made him unhappy to work in the fields. He was tall and handsome, intelligent and interesting, but very shy. When he finally got up enough courage to ask her to marry him, she lost no time in accepting.

Julian told her that he had been hired to take a large group of Indians to St. Louis for the World's Fair. They would be part of an Indian village that would dance, make pottery, and show visitors what Indians were like. This excited Maria's interest and she looked forward to going. It would be her first long trip from home.

In preparation for the wedding, Maria's home was

cleaned and whitewashed and food was prepared for the wedding feast. Every day, Maria ground corn into a fine meal and carried this to her mother-in-law in a basket. This was part of the wedding ritual. After the Indian marriage ceremony, the young couple were married again the next day by the Catholic priest.

In St. Louis, Julian learned to speak English. Maria already could. She made pottery and Julian decorated it, and they did well with sales. When they returned to San Ildefonso, Julian manfully worked for Tomas in the fields, and Maria's first child was born. His name was Adam.

Farming that year was discouraging. There were severe floods and the crops were drowned in the fields. Nobody went hungry, for it was the custom of the people to share and share alike. There was little to go around, but as Indians say, even a kernel of corn can be divided among several, and nobody complained. Julian, however, grew depressed and unhappy. He felt that he was a failure at farming.

Maria's second child, a daughter, was given her name —Poveka, or Yellow Pond Lily. Julian, by now, had been hired by a group of archaeologists to help them dig at one of the cliff dwelling ruins. This work interested him and he was especially careful in handling the objects found and in sifting the earth. His employers were pleased with him. But while he was away, Poveka died.

Julian gave all the money that he had earned to Maria when he returned home in the fall. He had been paid in silver dollars. According to custom, the money had to be shared with Maria's family and his parents. Tomas and Reyes now had three married daughters and one single one. Their other daughters' husbands who had also worked at the dig, had to share their money in the same way.

Maria gave Julian's parents more than hers, because

there was no one else to share with them. Tomas and Reyes divided the harvest from the fields, also—some to each daughter and some to Julian's parents. And Julian's father shared from his earnings, too.

One of the silver dollars Maria gave to Julian, and she put the rest of the money away for later use. Unfortunately, Julian, seeking relaxation after the months away, spent the money on drink and came home in a bad condition.

Maria was frightened and grieved. She hoped that this was only a single lapse, and perhaps due to Julian's grief over Poveka. But she feared that it might become a habit, and she had seen the tragic results among others who had done so. Perhaps it was too lonely for Julian at the dig. The next summer she went with him to the camp and did the cooking for the workers.

This time, the startling discovery of a buried city with a kiva and many artifacts and pieces of pottery was made. Some of the pottery was decorated. A painting of a water snake on a wall of a cave was a symbol of the rain god.

Maria and Julian were enchanted with these discoveries. With considerable artistic skill, Julian copied the snake symbol and other designs found in the ruins. He and Maria asked many questions about all that was found, and the director of the dig learned that Maria could make very fine pottery.

This was unusual, for the women of San Ildefonso no longer carried on pottery making. Pottery, when it was made, was purely functional. There was no concern for its appearance or even that it was made well. A bowl would be fashioned only when there was a need for it.

Sometimes the women would make small bowls for sale to tourists. After all the effort that was put into the work and the firing, they would walk twenty-two miles to Santa Fe and place their wares for sale on a sidewalk.

It was considered a good day if a woman made as much as fifty cents. But at last that was given up, too.

Maria, however, had never made any but the finest pots because that was how she was trained. She would not waste time on the inferior pieces that were turned out at the Pueblo.

At the dig, a set of small, hard, highly polished stones was found in one of the caves. Maria knew what they were. They were used to polish pottery. She could tell much about them for she used such stones herself. Sometimes a sheep bone was used, but the hard stones were much the best. Maria longed for a pair like these, but everything had to be turned over to the museum sponsoring the dig.

Scratching around in the caves, she soon found another pair and these she was allowed to keep. She fingered the stones over and over. If only they could talk— yet, in a way, they did. They made the ruins and the people who had lived there centuries before real to her.

A woman just like me used these, she thought. "She made pottery and polished it lovingly with these stones. May the stones give me her skill."

When the dig was over for that season, Maria and Julian returned to San Ildefonso. Maria worked at restoring the fragments of a bowl that had been entrusted to her. She became more and more interested in form and shape while Julian became interested in the designs and decoration.

How carefully she worked at the delicate task. The museum would pay well for the finished piece and perhaps they would give her others to do. She might also make some pieces of her own, and if they were unusually well done, the museum might buy them. Julian could decorate the new pottery, but with designs that came from the age-old ones.

In the old customs, the men had nothing to do with

pottery making. But Julian was to change all this. He made the work of pottery decorating acceptable to the men, opening up new employment for them. This was a major change in the social order, and a revolutionary one with respect to the craft.

When it came time for the dig to open up again, the museum gave Maria a good sum of money for the completed bowl. It was agreed that she would stay at the Pueblo and make more like the fine pieces the museum had purchased. In the winter months, Julian would decorate them, and the museum would buy every one, for they could readily sell it. They would build up a reputation for Maria's work and collectors of good Indian craft would want it.

In a way, Maria was glad to stay at home. Her mother had died, leaving a new baby to be cared for, and Maria, too, had a new child named Juan. But she worried about Julian. As she had feared it would, his drinking had become a habit and was growing worse. The men who drank caused hardship in the Pueblo and for their families. The village was so small, that every man was needed to do his share of the work.

While Julian was at the dig, he would not drink. If he could keep busy doing what he liked to do when he returned, Maria thought, perhaps the drinking could be controlled. Perhaps he drank because of the field work that he hated.

So, under her nimble fingers, more than two hundred beautiful bowls piled up waiting for Julian to come home. When he did, he had exciting news. He had been asked to work at the museum in Santa Fe as janitor. There would be two rooms in the museum where they could live and they could make and sell pottery to museum visitors.

Maria was not happy at this news. She did not like to live in a city. But then, Julian was not happy at farming and when he married her he had farmed and carried out the responsibility to his family. She had a responsibility to Julian. She said that she would go.

Life in Santa Fe, for the three years that Maria and Julian lived there, was very different from that at San Ildefonso. With only two rooms to care for, there was little housework to do. Julian had time to study the designs on the bowls in the pottery collection, and he would tell Maria about them. She began to visit the museum and to wander among the exhibits and she, too, began to study the ancient vessels of such fine craftsmanship and intricate design. Her sensitivity to pottery making was stirred. She talked about the pottery with Julian and with the museum director who encouraged her to try to reproduce some of the older pieces. He showed her some bits of a highly polished black ware that had been found in the Pueblo ruins. None of the Pueblo people knew anything about it.

The black pottery stayed in Maria's mind. If she could find a way to make it she would have something to give to her people. Perhaps they would turn to pottery making again.

Maria now followed a quest. She experimented with clays, with sand, with firing. She tried again and again, but the black ware was elusive. She failed so often that she wanted to give up, but Julian encouraged her to go on.

So much of Maria's other pottery had been sold that they now had money in the bank and could anticipate income from continued sales. They decided to return to San Ildefonso and go into the pottery business. They built an addition to their home for a small store where they could sell supplies to the Indians and where they could have a workshop to make and sell pottery.

The experiments went on and then, completely by accident, Maria learned that the black finish was produced by firing. Some years before, when making pottery for the museum, two of her bowls had come out black. Thinking they were spoiled, she had put them away and forgotten about them.

Quickly the bowls were brought out and while Maria tried to remember what she had done, Julian tried to find the way to do it again. At first, the bowls came out a shiny red. Then Julian discovered what was needed to produce the black ones, and a new style in pottery making was born.

The bowls, however, could not be decorated. Any decoration that was applied vanished when the pottery was fired. Again, Maria spent long hours in patient effort and at last produced a fluid that came out of the firing like dull etching against the polished lustre of the pottery. It was black on black, like a black moire.

The new pottery was as fine and as perfect as Maria's hands and Julian's brush could make it. No pottery wheel was ever used, yet each bowl was in absolute balance. Everyone wanted the black bowls, it seemed. The traders would order in large quantities, and Maria could barely keep up with the demand.

Julian was more content, although the drinking never ceased entirely. He could give free rein to his skill and he excelled in the imaginative creation of birds, animals, and other creatures, and the application of ancient designs and figures. His favorite designs were the plumed serpent and the sun symbol. The designs were drawn entirely freehand without a ruler or a pattern to follow, and they were always in perfect harmony and balance.

Maria felt that now she could teach the other women of the Pueblo this unusual black-on-black craft. She was a strict teacher who tolerated nothing but meticulous work. The pottery was too beautiful to be spoiled by imperfections. It was unique and therefore must be kept as something quite special—something that belonged to

San Ildefonso alone. She would accept no one as a pupil who was not willing to conform to this ideal of perfection.

Julian, too, became a teacher. He taught the men how to decorate the pottery and about the rhythm of design and what design looked best on the various pottery shapes. Maria had turned her attention to making tall vases and plates, or plaques, and these, too, became a craft tradition. She also made a prancing horse.

All of the pottery for sale was placed on open display without being identified as the work of a particular artist. But is was Maria's work that was constantly asked for. To save them having to continually assure buyers as to authenticity, it was suggested that Maria and Julian sign each of their pieces. This would also make the work more valuable.

Julian could not write, so Maria traced his name for him and he learned to copy it. The signatures were written with a piece of stone before the pottery was fired. Such pieces, today, are extremely valuable.

Naturally, the autographed pieces sold first. Maria and Julian, fearing that this would hurt the sales of the other makers, then offered to sign everyone's pottery. This was in the true Pueblo spirit, which held all to an equal level and prevented any one individual from getting ahead of another. It was done out of an unselfish motive, but it defeated the purpose of the signature. Again, it was only by the perfection of the work that a buyer could be certain it was a piece of Maria's pottery. At last, the other workers began to sign their pieces with their own names and that ended the confusion.

San Ildefonso now had a thriving industry that brought in a higher income than that of farming. A new era had come.

Maria's pottery, entered in art shows and exhibits, won many awards and was eagerly sought by museums and private collectors not only here but abroad. There is some of her work in nearly every major art museum.

After three years of prize winning, she said she would accept no more awards. "They are to go to the other Indian woman," she said, "so that they will be encouraged to keep on producing good work."

In 1934, she and Julian were asked to appear at the Century of Progress in Chicago. At this time, she was presented the Indian Achievement Award, the second person and the first woman to receive it. The award was initiated with the opening of the exposition in 1933 by the Indian Council Fire, a national Indian-interest organization. It was the only national recognition given to Indians at that time, and has remained the highest in stature since. The first award was presented to Dr. Charles A. Eastman, a Sioux physician, author, and lecturer.

Thousands of people witnessed the presentation to Maria and stood to honor her as the bronze medallion, designed by a Cherokee artist, was placed in her hand. Among those taking part in the program was another famous Indian woman. This was Daisy Maude Underwood, a Chickasaw from Oklahoma, who was gaining fame as an operatic singer.

Maria received many other honors after that, among them an honorary doctorate from the University of Colorado, an award from the American Institute of Architects, the Jane Addams Award from Rockford College, an award from the American Ceramic Society, and another from the Minnesota Museum of Art. She was also recognized by the French Government with the bestowal of the *Ordre des Palmes Académiques* in special ceremonies held in Santa Fe.

Maria and Julian attended a number of expositions after this, and once they went on a long demonstration trip with a group of Indians. It took them across the country and Julian collected samples of clay from every state they passed through. Maria made bowls of different shapes from each bit of clay and Julian decorated them with exquisite designs. Each one is a gem and the entire collection is on display in the museum at Albuquerque.

Maria enjoyed all of the trips. She liked meeting people, but best of all, Julian did not drink when he was away from home. Each trip was a happy experience.

Once back at San Ildefonso, Julian's affliction worsened. The oldest son in the family, Adam, had to help Maria raise the two younger boys, Tony and Philip, for Julian was so often unable to function. Adam was living in the traditional way. Juan, or John as he was now called, was an engineering graduate from Stanford University and lived away from the Pueblo.

When the last two boys were grown, Julian was elected governor of San Ildefonso. He was a most intelligent and capable man, and he was a creditable governor, in spite of his problem. During World War II he was in charge of signing up the young men of the Pueblo for the draft. All of his sons had to register. Philip, who was still in school, insisted upon volunteering and enlisted in the Navy. Adam, who was needed at home, was the only one of the Martinez boys who was not in the service.

In 1943, Julian wandered away from the Pueblo and was not heard of for several days. Then he was found on a hill above the village, dead of exposure. He was buried secretly in the Indian way, but a Catholic mass was later held for him.

For a while, Maria was too crushed to work. Julian had held her to her course when she had been too discouraged to continue. Although it was she who had raised not only her family but the entire Pueblo to prosperity and to better standards, it was Julian upon whom she had leaned. He had helped greatly and her story cannot be told without him.

But not for long could she remain idle. She had a business to run, a store to manage, and pottery orders to fill. Tony, who used the name of Popovi Da began to work with his mother. He had Julian's artistic talent, and he was very popular in the Pueblo. He was several times chosen governor.

With Tony, Maria turned once more to research. She developed a new slip, or finish, which gave a gunmetal sheen—almost a silver overlay—to the ebony lustre of her pottery, softening and mellowing it.

Mother and son worked well together, and the bowls bore a different autograph—Maria and Popovi Da. But as she entered her mid-eighties, Maria did not work as much. She lived in her comfortable hillside home and watched the changing life of the village. Her life, too, had changed so much since the time of her marriage. A book had been written about her, and several films produced. While she had seen much of the outside world, she dressed always in Pueblo clothing with her hair in traditional Pueblo fashion. She was looked up to as the Mother of the Pueblo, a title of great respect. Many people came to the Pueblo, hoping to meet her, but she did not talk with many people, now.

Of her twenty-four great-grandchildren, some are potters and live at San Ildefonso; others have entered nursing and electronics and Maria finds no fault with this. "There is a place for both," she says, and "they will go where their place is."

Popovi Da died in 1972 and this was another crushing blow to survive. Now in her nineties, her mind alive with memories, she looks back on a life that shines with service as her pottery shines with beauty. She lives quietly from one day to the next, completely unspoiled by the attention and honor that has been given her, serene in the knowledge that has preserved and upheld tradition— living in today but remaining in the Pueblo circle of love, understanding, and sharing.

ANNIE DODGE WAUNEKA

A MODERN CRUSADER

Annie Dodge Wauncka is a Navajo. The Navajos are the largest tribe in the country. Their vast reservation sprawls over twenty-five thousand square miles in New Mexico, Arizona, Utah, and Colorado. There are mountain peaks capped with crowns of snow, towering twelve thousand feet above the land. There are strange, centuries old rock formations, deep red, orange, and yellow. There are long stretches of desert and shadowy canyons. There are pine forests, grazing lands, and areas of planted fields.

Since the coming of the Spaniards many years ago, the Navajos have been shepherds and horsemen. The women weave beautiful rugs from the wool of their sheep and have developed weaving to a fine art. The men are skilled in silver work, producing some of the finest jewelry found anywhere.

Although they have taken on a good deal in the way of American customs, the Navajos still follow much of their traditional way of life. Ancient ceremonies are kept alive and Indian clothes are worn, especially by the women. Many of the people prefer to live in the Navajo style house—a low round building of log walls plastered with mud. There is a smokehole at the top of the roof and a fire in the center of the floor. There are no windows and no furniture, or very little. The house, which looks something like a beehive, is called a hogan.

It was in such a house that Annie was born on an April day in 1910. The hogan belonged to her mother.

Annie's father was the noted Henry Chee Dodge, one of the greatest of Navajo leaders. When he was still a child, the Navajos were rounded up by the army because they had been raiding the white settlements that encroached on their lands. Their fields were burned, their houses destroyed. Forced to walk more than three hundred miles across the desert, they were taken as prisoners to Fort Sumner and kept there four years.

Chee Dodge was separated from his family and never saw them again. He was a favorite at the army post and learned to speak English. Soon he was acting as an interpreter for the army officials.

When the Navajos were finally returned to their homes, Chee Dodge went with them, still an army interpreter. By the time he was twenty, he was official interpreter for the government. He would study a dictionary to learn about words and their exact meanings, for he had come to know that English words did not always mean what Indians thought they meant.

By the time Annie was born, Chee had become wealthy. He was a rancher and lived in a fine house with many rooms and luxurious furnishings. More and more he was called upon to act as adviser to his people.

Following Navajo custom, Chee married two sisters. Later he married a distant relation of theirs. It was this wife who was Annie's mother.

When she was a year old, Chee took Annie to live with him in the big house. She had two half-brothers and a half-sister. As she grew older, she began to see that her father was very important. He was a strong leader, a good business man, and no other Navajo had ever been so wealthy. Annie's growing up years with her father were to shape her whole life.

When she was five, she cared for her stepmother's sheep and goats. This, too, was Navajo custom. The children learned very early to do the work that was expected of them. Every day at sunrise, she took the flock to the foothills near her home to graze. If a lamb was lost, she hunted for it, carrying it back to the flock in her strong arms.

Annie had sheep of her own, too. Her father added to her personal flock each year when the lambs were born. Annie would be a wealthy woman in her own right.

Annie loved the sheep. Although she was alone with them all day, she was never lonely. She talked to the sheep and sang songs to them. They clustered around her sure that she would keep them safe from harm.

When it was bright morning, Annie returned with the flock to the house. The family gathered around a table for breakfast. Although they ate Navajo style, with the food in one bowl from which each person helped himself, they did not otherwise live like Navajos. The customs of the Dodge home were more white than Indian.

Many guests came to see Chee Dodge, and then the food was served on good china and with silver tableware. Annie took great interest in the distinguished people who visited her father. But, even though he went far in the white man's world, his life was lived for his people. He influenced them always for their own betterment, and the Navajos did not resent his wealth or importance though it was not their way for one to be stronger or richer than others.

Nobody lingered at breakfast, for there was always work waiting on the ranch. Annie returned with the flock to the foothills, taking her lunch with her. As little as she was, her family trusted her to carry out this task. She watched to see that the animals did not eat poisonous plants or the dread "loco weed" which drove them crazy. She watched, too, that they did not overeat and that they had water.

Navajo children, at that time, seldom went to school. Since there were almost no schools on the reservation the children had to go far from their homes to boarding schools run by the government. Some went to mission schools. When they came home ceremonies were held to cleanse them of evil spirits. The Navajos believed that those who went away from the tribe had to be cured of outside influences.

Chee Dodge, however, had no such feelings. He sent all of his children to white schools. He wanted them to have the education that he did not have.

When Annie was eight, she was sent to the government school at Fort Defiance. In that year, the reservation was hit by a terrible influenza epidemic. Thousands of the people died. At the school there was only one nurse to care for the children, many of whom died, too.

Annie tried to be helpful. Every morning she cleaned and filled at least one hundred kerosene lanterns that were used at night. She fed soup to the sick ones and bathed their faces with cool cloths.

Not long after this, there was another terrible epidemic. This time it was a serious eye condition leading to blindness. Indians were especially subject to it. With other children, Annie had to be sent to another school to avoid infection.

Both of these experiences made a strong impression upon her. She wondered why the Navajos had so much poor health and what could be done about it. She thought about becoming a nurse. She wanted to help those who were suffering and she had no fear of becoming ill herself.

In the spring when the lambs were born, Annie went home. Everyone on the ranch had to help with the lambing, for Chee Dodge had very large flocks. He could have hired someone to do Annie's work. But, among the Navajos it is the women who take care of the sheep giving birth. Annie must follow Navajo tradition in this.

When the government school at Albuquerque was opened for the first time to Navajo students, Annie was sent there. Since there were also children from other tribes at the school, English was spoken constantly. Annie learned quickly. She was an excellent student and soon was on a level with the older children.

While she was at Albuquerque, Chee Dodge was elected chairman of the tribe. The Navajos had never had chiefs, only head men. Now, for the first time in their history they had a business council with a chairman responsible for tribal government.

Once Annie's father came to Albuquerque to speak to the children. He told them how important it was to get an education—as much as possible. Twelve-year-old Annie sat very straight and her eyes shone with pride for her father. She listened to his words with deepening understanding. She did not return home again until she was eighteen and her education was completed.

Between Annie and her father, a special bond grew up. Her half-brother, Tom, was away at college preparing to be a lawyer. He was to become the first attorney of Navajo blood, and later he would become tribal chairman like his father. Chee's other children were married with interests of their own.

So it was Annie on whom Chee relied. He had her help with interpreting, insisting that she know the exact meaning of words, as he had learned them. He looked to her to carry on his ideals and teachings, for he recognized her strength of character. In turn, Annie respected her father for his fairness and strong sense of justice. Although he was no longer chairman of the council, he was as busy as ever. He was the one to whom the people turned when they wanted guidance.

Annie now traveled over the reservation with her father, into areas where she had never been. She saw a side of life that she had not known existed. She saw great poverty and much illness. More than ever, she came to understand why her father said that education was the only way to solve Indian needs.

Annie departed from Navajo custom to choose her own husband—George Wauneka, who had been a schoolmate of hers at Albuquerque. Her wedding was an important social event because of her father's position. The Waunekas, too, were a highly respected family. The wedding itself was entirely in accord with Navajo custom. Annie was dressed in Navajo style—full skirts, velveteen blouse, much silver and turquoise jewelry, hair pulled back and tied with yarn. This is the type of dress she wears today. Standing nearly six feet tall, she is proudly Navajo wherever she goes.

Chee Dodge gave the Waunekas a comfortable home on one of his ranches, turning this property and the management of his cattle herds, over to them. Annie had eight children, two of whom died.

In spite of the demands on her time made by the ranch and her family, she still accompanied her father to tribal meetings. She went with him to the hogans of those who asked for help. Her heart went out to those who were in poor health or were hungry, for her own children were growing up well and strong.

At Fort Defiance, the sick children had been kept clean and away from others, she remembered. In the hogans, the floors were of dirt, as they always had been. With little water, they were hard to keep clean. Water had to be brought in barrels by wagons from great distances. Both sick and well lived and slept together.

Annie wanted to make things better for these Navajos. She began to speak out against dirt floors and a lack of cleanliness. Sometimes this made the people angry. Sometimes they listened.

Navajo flocks and herds had become a great problem. They had grown too large for the land to support. Pastures were overgrazed and the topsoil washed away when it rained. The government said that the Navajos must cut down on their sheep, goats, cattle, and horses. To the Navajos, this was an outrage. To have to part with their animals, they felt, was a disaster.

Chee Dodge had to explain why the government order had been given. He understood that the reasons were right and that the action was necessary. Hundreds of his own animals would have to be sacrificed, but his concern was for those who could not stand the loss. He knew what a blow this was to his people.

Chee told the Navajos that the government was acting for, not against them. The government had saved the Navajos, he said, when they were nearly destroyed by their enemies, the Utes and the Comanches. When they had returned from Fort Sumner with nothing but the rags they wore, the government had given each Navajo two sheep to start a flock. The two had grown to a thousand, he said. The Navajos had always done what was asked of them and they must do so again. It was for their good.

Annie listened to her father with awe and admiration. To her it was a tremendous speech—but not to the other Navajos. They heard it with deep anger and bitterness.

Until he died at the age of eighty-six, not once did Chee Dodge ever speak out against the government policy or the idea behind it. The Navajos were not independent and it would be some time before they could be entirely free of government control. This would come only with education.

After his death, Annie continued to carry on her father's work. She so won the trust and affection of her people that her community elected her to represent them as delegate to the tribal council. This was a long step forward, for she was the first woman ever chosen by the Navajos for such a position. Until then, it was only the men who made the decisions. And now the men had given her a voice and a vote in council proceedings.

Those who knew Annie knew that she would not be at all backward about stating her opinions and that she would vote as she thought best. She was every inch the daughter of Chee Dodge. She made her presence felt, as he did.

It was unusual that Chee and Annie were of such influence. Among Indians, individual power has not been encouraged. It is the group that is important. Indians are suspicious of personal success, thinking that the successful one may be using witchcraft.

Chee, in his lifetime, acquired great wealth. Annie both inherited and acquired wealth on her own. Chee did not live as a Navajo, but almost like a feudal lord. He went against Navajo custom in many things, but always he respected the feelings of the people. He did not try to force them to change, but tried instead to persuade them by example.

Annie follows this same pattern. In her life style, both old and new are blended. Her home is a long way from any town. She has no phone and must drive thirty miles to get her mail. Her house is tastefully furnished with fine Navajo rugs on the floors and walls. She works around the ranch with the men, cares for the sheep and the cattle, and rides horseback over her extensive property. She is as at home on a plane as she is on a horse.

She speaks Navajo at home and when she visits her

people. She respects tradition and practices some of the old religious ceremonies. She encourages Navajo young people to appreciate the good and the beautiful in the Navajo way of life so that it will not be lost to them forever.

Because she has much, she is expected to be generous with those who have little, and she is. Over and over she demonstrates her dedication to Navajo welfare. Never does she say it is wrong to think or act like a Navajo. She says, let us find a better way to help ourselves, keeping what is right for us from our own and taking from others what will help us the most.

When Annie was elected to the Council, the men did not know quite how to deal with her. Finally, they appointed her chairman of the health committee and she lost no time in getting to work.

She proposed to do battle against tuberculosis, the greatest killer on the reservation. She knew she faced a hard task because of the Indians' fear of white doctors and hospitals. Tribal medicine men would not welcome that which would weaken their position in the tribal structure.

To fight believably, she must know as much about tuberculosis as it was possible for her to know. First, she went to the reservation's government doctors and asked to be taught about TB. She wanted all of the facts on the cause so she could explain them, and she wanted as much information as possible on treatment, so she could interpret it. The doctors were glad to cooperate with her.

For three months, she studied in the hospitals and laboratories run by the U. S. Public Health Service. She looked into microscopes, checked X rays, watched patients. When she had found out all that she could, she began to visit tubercular Indian patients in hospitals. She told them in language they could understand what was wrong with them and what was being done for them. This meant that she had to make up some new words, for there were none in the Navajo language for some of the things she had to tell about.

Next, she talked with the medicine men. She had no desire to anger them, for their cooperation was necessary. To the Navajos, the medicine man is both priest and doctor who heals with ceremonies. So strongly did the people believe in the ceremonies that without them they often did not get well.

Annie talked with the medicine men about the old ways. She pointed out that TB was an "outside" disease and that many became ill with it the world over. The powers of the medicine man might not be strong enough to overcome something of this kind, she said. The medicine men and the white doctors should combine their skills and work together. Miraculously, she was able to bring this about. Today, the medicine men and the doctors work in harmonious partnership.

Next, she wrote a book which listed Navajo medical terms in English and English medical terms in Navajo. This was a monumental task, especially for one whose schooling did not go beyond eleventh grade.

Turning her attention to those who were sick, she went to the family hogan when she heard of illness and urged that the sick one be put in a hospital. Many such trips were made. She did not give anyone a chance to change their minds once they had agreed. She took the sick one back to the hospital with her, or arranged for transportation. She stayed with the patients as if they were her own, soothing their fears and comforting them. She visited patients, carried messages back and forth, and constantly sustained morale.

She sought out those who had run away from the hospital, too, and persuaded them to return. Because of Annie, twenty thousand Navajos reported for X rays and more than 2,000 were hospitalized in a short time. More hospitals and clinics were opened on the reservation as the reluctance to use them dwindled. All Navajos received free medical care.

Annie extended her efforts. She acted in and helped to produce two movies on health. For two years, she had her own radio program, talking to the people in Navajo about a wide range of health subjects. She asked the council for money for wooden floors and windows for every hogan. When this was refused, nothing daunted, she toured the reservation campaigning for this project. The council finally acted and allowed $300,000—not enough, but at least a partial victory and a start.

In Annie's lifetime, many changes have taken place on the reservation and she has played an important part directly, or an influential one indirectly, in bringing them about.

Going to the hospital has become an accepted way of life among the people. It is commonplace, now, for babies to be born there. The Tribal Council has contributed funds to support TB research within the tribe. TB is no longer the "killer" and the death rate from other diseases has been sharply reduced. Navajo children are given shots and polio vaccination in their schools. Navajos have been recruited to the health profession— among them two of Annie's daughters who are public health workers.

Many Navajos are in college and a number have gone on to graduate schools. They are found in all walks of professional and vocational life. A $10 million scholarship fund is maintained by the tribe for the use of their young people. Navajo parents are beginning to take over the management of their schools, and the tribe has built its own college. Tribal enterprises are run by Navajos.

More and more Navajos have moved from the hogan into small, modest homes. The hogan may stand nearby for ceremonial use.

Civic activities and programs of various kinds take place. Boy Scouts and Girl Scout troops flourish on the reservation. There are fewer horses and more cars and pickup trucks. There is an Indian-owned supermarket and there are luxury motels to attract tourists.

Fame and honor have come to Annie's door from health and civic organizations the country over. In 1959, the Arizona Press Women named her "Woman of the Year" and she received the Indian Achievement Award, a national recognition given to Indian people by an Indian-interest organization. In 1963, she received the highest recognition of all. This was the Freedom Award given by President Kennedy to only a few outstanding citizens, and presented by President Johnson after Kennedy's death.

This award is always pinned to Annie's blouse, for it was a very great honor. Because of it, the Navajos speak of her as the Badge Woman.

But she has another name—one that goes far back into Navajo tradition. It is Warrior Who Scouts the Enemy. What name could be more appropriate? She scouted the enemy of health and like a true warrior fought to overcome those conditions that were destroying her people.

ESTHER BURNETT HORNE

SACAJAWEA'S
GREAT-GREAT-GRANDDAUGHTER

"The wonderful thing about having an illustrious ances-tor is the inspiration that is so constantly before you to do and become." This has been the philosophy of Esther Burnett Horne from the time of her childhood when she first learned of her relationship to Sacajawea, the girl who acted as guide for the Lewis and Clark Expedition.

Esther, with Sacajawea's story as a reminder, set out to become a guide and trail blazer for other Indian young people, concentrating all her young efforts toward that goal.

Her grandfather, Finn Burnett, could tell her much about Sacajawea, for he knew her well. Finn was an-other who helped to make history. He was a frontiers-man who rode with Jim Bridger and fought beside the great Shoshone, Chief Washakie. It is said that Finn did more to elevate the Shoshones at Wind River and to help them become self-supporting than any other individual.

Sacajawea taught Finn how to speak Shoshone, and he worked with her, her son Baptiste, whom she had car-ried on her back to the Pacific, and her adopted son,

Bazil, in teaching the Shoshones to till the soil and raise wheat. As a result, the tribe had the first flour mill in Wyoming.

Esther was born at Fort Washakie, but spent the first eleven years of her life near Twin Falls, Idaho. Her father was a fruit farmer, who also raised sugar beets and had a small cattle herd.

Esther would drive the hay wagon while her father threw off hay for the animals. She rode horseback over the farm, swam in the irrigation ditches, and helped with the fruit picking and packing. It was a busy, happy childhood.

Both her parents stressed cultural patterns repeatedly to their six children. To be a good Indian was to be a good person, they said. The responsibility to do the right thing in the right place and at the right time because you had the individual strength to do it was instilled into her character and was an integral part of her thinking.

When Esther's father died her mother returned with the children to the reservation where she later remarried. Esther's love for her father was profound, and it was difficult, at first, to adjust to a stepfather. Reservation living was also very different from the non-Indian community in which she had grown up. Everyone was related in some way, and this meant that everything had to be shared, and there was little to share. It was hard to keep track of the relationships, too. There were some people to whom you could speak only in a certain way and with whom you must not laugh or joke. This had to be remembered. There were some, too, who were not related at all by blood, yet in the Indian way of calculating were closely related.

One day, Esther's mother took her children to the Indian cemetery and pointed out a grave—the grave of Sacajawea. The children were told the Sacajawea story and Esther could never hear it enough. She began to look up to her great-great-grandmother almost as an idol. She thought about her often. What courage she must have had! From then on, she modeled her life on Sacajawea's.

At night, with supper over and the dishes put away, she would beg to hear about Sacajawea again, asking many questions about what she had looked like, what she had said, and what she did. She was told that when she was young, Sacajawea was small, rather light-complexioned, and quite pretty. She was a gentle, smiling person, spoke mostly in French, and was pleasant to everyone. Those who knew, said that Esther strongly resembled her. She is of about the same size and build, with the same attractive face and gentle manner.

Many times, Esther revisited the grave. In the summer, the hills of Wyoming are covered with a brightly colored flower called Indian Paint Brush. Esther was named in Indian for this flower. She would gather small bouquets of it and place them on the grave, with the comforting thought that Sacajawea would know she had done so and would be pleased. She must have loved the flower as I do, she thought.

As she added to her store of knowledge about Sacajawea, Esther told herself that she would try always to be worthy of her. That she, too, would "walk in her moccasins," and become noteworthy, for this would be the best way to honor one so close and so famous. It would be unthinkable to behave in a way that would tarnish that wonderful name.

When it was time to go to high school, Esther was sent away to Haskell Indian School at Lawrence, Kansas, a government-operated boarding school. At school, she was often asked to pose for pictures publicizing Haskell because of her Sacajawea relationship. She spoke before churches, clubs, and service groups, telling about Sacajawea, and about Indians and the need for an education, and this gave her a poise and an insight beyond her years.

Esther had always liked school and was a good student. Coming from a socially and economically deprived background, as did most of the Haskell young people, she would have had no opportunity to continue with her schooling if it had not been for the Haskell experience.

The plan was that the students attended classes one-half day and worked for the institution one-half day. The girls worked in the laundry and the sewing room. The school was run by military discipline, and the students were divided into military companies and wore uniforms. Some were appointed company officers and were involved in establishing the rules and regulations to a limited extent.

In the junior and senior years, business and other professional courses were offered, and Esther chose teacher's training. She was helped to make this decision by two well-loved teachers, Ruth Muskrat Bronson, a Cherokee, and Ella Deloria, a Sioux. Both strongly influenced her life. It was felt that through teaching she could help her people the most, for there was a tremendous need for Indian teachers.

From Haskell, Esther went immediately to teach at a boarding school for Creek Indian girls at Eufaula, Oklahoma. Then she was sent to the Wahpeton Boarding School in North Dakota, where she remained for thirty years. During that time, she married Robert Horne, a Hoopa Indian from California, who had been a schoolmate at Haskell and was also employed at Wahpeton.

Esther proved to be a highly creative teacher with an inner zeal given to a rare few. Her prime purpose was to show her children what contributions their race had made to civilization. She wanted them to take pride in the early Indians who were people of accomplishment, not crude wild people as they were so often portrayed. She told them that one of their own was considered one of the six greatest women produced in the United States, and that person was Sacajawea.

This was not done through any sense of self-aggrandizement, but to help Indian youth have a feeling of belonging and of equality. "If for two moons you walk in another's moccasins, you will learn that all people are the same," she said.

In her classes, she emphasized the virtues of Indian culture by teaching Indian values and how Indians did things before the white man came. They had an effective civilization, and from them, the whites learned many things. She made history come to life, not only in her classroom, but through three historical pageants, which she wrote and directed and in which her students acted the parts.

Sacajawea was an expert in Indian sign language, so it is not surprising that Esther taught it, too, as part of her Indian culture studies. She trained her students to "speak" the Twenty-Third Psalm in this beautiful, expressive hand-talk, and this presentation was copied by other Indian students elsewhere. It is frequently given on Indian programs today.

She directed her efforts toward the dignity of each individual student, helping each to feel a security and confidence in his ability to be as successful as any other person.

"Sacajawea was said to have had a 'nameless charm,'" she pointed out. "Much of her beauty and charm came from within and it was born of the Indian serenity of spirit."

Her two daughters, Yvonne and Diane, were brought up to have the same reverence for Sacajawea that their mother had. One of her daughters, when grown, posed for a new statue of Sacajawea that was to be erected in Bismarck, North Dakota.

Naturally drawn to the Girl Scout movement because it seemed to embody much of the Sacajawea concept, Esther organized the first Indian Girl Scout troop in the United States and she has worked actively with Girl Scouts throughout her life.

Esther and her husband took many children from broken homes and other disadvantaged children into their home and helped them to go on with their education. Esther kept in touch with all of these young people, writing them inspirational letters and following their lives with interest and compassion.

In 1955, she was selected to act as the guide for the 1956 Lewis and Clark Return Expedition, representing her great-great grandmother. For this she wore Shoshone costume with a replica around her neck of the medal which Lewis and Clark gave to Indian chiefs they met along the way. She spoke to thousands of people en route, once again telling the story of Sacajawea and of her return to the Wind River Reservation. This was part of the Sesquicentennial Expedition—the 150th commemoration of the Lewis and Clark journey.

Among the observations was the dedication of a number of markers along the Lewis and Clark trail and the unveiling of a bust of Sacajawea at the original site where the expedition party spent their first winter and where it was agreed that Sacajawea and her husband would travel with the party. Esther was the model for this bust.

Three years later, she was present at the placement of another commemorative statue of Sacajawea in the Indian Hall of Fame at Anadarko, Oklahoma. While there, she was honored by the governor of the state and made an honorary lieutenant governor.

In 1965, Esther visited ten different countries as "North Dakota's Good Will Ambassador" promoting European travel to this country and an interest in genuine Indian arts and crafts. She met such dignitaries as Charles de Gaulle and Willy Brandt, and even went behind the Iron Curtain into East Berlin.

Shortly before her retirement from teaching, Esther Horne was given the Distinguished Service Award in Education by the Department of the Interior. The Distinguished Service Award gold medal, the highest honor conferred by the department, acknowledged her singular leadership and noteworthy contribution, exemplifying the highest type of teaching both in the classroom and in associated areas of teaching.

Retirement did not mean inactivity, however. She has continued as an educational consultant, and she returned once more to Wahpeton to officiate at the dedication of Sacajawea Hall, a new dormitory for girls. She has had published many articles on Indian culture and education and has completed the manuscript for a book entitled "Materials for the Development of a Better Understanding of Indian Americans." She was also cited as an outstanding alumna of Haskell Indian Junior College, selected by the school's alumni throughout the nation.

She keeps busy with church and club work, family and home, teaches Indian folk dancing and singing and continues to be a guide and a force for good.

THE TALLCHIEF SISTERS

PRIMA BALLERINAS

Maria and Marjorie Tallchief have risen to the pinnacle of the world of the performing arts—the first Indian women who have excelled in an art in which few others have achieved comparable stature.

Maria Tallchief is considered one of the world's greatest ballerinas, in the opinion of some critics surpassing such universally acclaimed dancers as the legendary Pavlova, Plisetskaya, and Fonteyn.

Marjorie, her sister, also ranks among the great and is a remarkably versatile dancer. She, too, has a glowing place in ballet history.

As children, the two girls lived with their parents and brother in a comfortable house on the Osage Indian reservation in Oklahoma. Maria, who was named Betty Marie, was born there. Marjorie was born in Denver.

Alexander Tall Chief, their father, was an Osage chief. Their mother was of Scotch-Irish ancestry. Their great-grandfather was Chief Bigheart who negotiated the treaty with the government that brought the Osages from Kansas to Oklahoma.

The Osages were one of the most important midwestern tribes. They had played a particularly important role in the growth of the United States, for they had been the buffer between the French, Spanish, and English who struggled to gain control over the middle part of the country. The Osages were always friendly to the Americans and with the completion of the Louisiana Purchase they continued to be so.

When the government established a policy that Indian tribes were to be removed to Indian Territory, land that would be reserved for Indians only, the Osages chose for themselves an area that was good hunting territory. They were primarily a hunting people and they did not want to be different. Then, to everybody's surprise, oil was discovered and the Osages became wealthy overnight. They were also catapulted into a completely new way of living. They built beautiful houses and rode in handsome cars driven by chauffeurs. Their young people went to exclusive schools and took trips to Europe. Indian traditions were thrown aside and Osage ways disappeared except for a remnant culture among the older people.

The Tall Chiefs were proud of being Osages, but if it were not for their grandmother who lived with them, they would have nothing of their Indian background. Grandmother Eliza Bigheart kept it alive with her stories of the old days and of the venerable chief who was her father.

Otherwise, Betty Marie and Marjorie grew up as any other children in a well-to-do home. They lived in the modern world of change and not in the traditional ways of their ancestors. They could speak not one word of Osage, for it was not used in their home; and they were remote from the older people who still observed Indian customs.

From the time they were very small, they were preparing for careers that had been planned for them. When Betty Marie was three, it was learned that she had perfect pitch, a rare musical ability, and that she was able to pick out simple tunes on the piano. Her mother, therefore, decided that Betty Marie would become a concert pianist and, as small as she was, her music lessons began at once.

Marjorie was to be a dancer. She was a lively child, active and lithe, and of an outgoing disposition. Betty Marie was grave and serious, very much in earnest about anything she undertook.

When Betty Marie was four, she began to take dancing lessons to "develop grace." Her teacher came to the home once a week and taught her to stand on her toes, to leap, and to spin about. When she was five, she appeared in her first dance recital. Dressed in a costume of red, white, and blue, and carrying an American flag, the beautiful child whirling about the stage was a sensation.

By this time, Marjorie was also embarked on dancing lessons, and she delighted in every minute of it, for it suited her active, light-hearted nature. Betty Marie was unsure whether she liked music or dancing the most. She did both in her usual do-or-die manner.

Although Betty Marie and Marjorie were a year apart in age, they looked so much alike they were often mistaken for twins. Their days were very full, but they had reached a point where they needed more and better training. They had gone as far as they could go in their home town of Fairfax, and so when Betty Marie was eight and Marjorie was seven, the Tall Chief family moved to Los Angeles where they lived in the suburb of Beverly Hills. Going to a new school was hard at first. The Indian name aroused a lot of curiosity, even snickers and would-be war whoops. But gradually this died down and the sisters were one of the crowd. Marjorie made friends easily, but Betty Marie was shy and reserved, and she had very little time for socializing.

Mrs. Tall Chief enrolled Betty Marie in music school at once, and both girls were registered for classes with a fine ballet teacher, Ernest Belcher. He was the best that Los Angeles could provide, and he was horrified when he first saw them dance.

They knew nothing of the rudiments of ballet or even the basic positions. He made them stop toe dancing at once, declaring it a miracle that their feet had not been damaged for life. He would not accept them as pupils unless they would agree to "un-learn" everything that they had been taught and start out as any other beginner. There would be no dancing until he said so.

Endless hours were spent in practice. Marjorie found this irking, but she stayed with it. Betty Marie, however, was absorbed by it all. She strove constantly for perfection and practice, to her, was a ritual.

Throughout her school days, Betty Marie practiced the piano twice a day—before going to school and as soon as she returned from school. As soon as the girls got up in the morning they exercised and reviewed their dancing lessons. At five o'clock in the evening they left for their ballet class which lasted two hours. After dinner, there was school homework to do and then to bed. It was a rugged schedule.

It was a welcome change when Mr. Belcher permitted them to dance in a school program. They were to dance an Indian number, because they were Indians, of course. It was anything but Indian, but it was dancing, so Betty Marie tried not to care. Marjorie was overjoyed with the dance. She carried a knife in her hand and brandished it about with energy. It was far better than the constant practicing.

When the program was over, everyone said "how fine," and "how interesting to see an Indian dance."

Betty Marie thought of the Osage dances at home. Sometimes her grandmother had taken her to see them. How the Osages would laugh at the Indian program!

When the sisters were ten and nine, Mr. Belcher chose them to perform in the ballet of the Los Angeles Opera Company. They did not have featured roles, of course, but it was a wonderful opportunity and their first professional appearance. Only the best pupils were given this chance.

This experience helped Betty Marie to know her own feelings better. She had been more and more torn between music and dancing. She was pulled by one and pushed by the other. For some time she had felt as though she were a double person and envied Majorie's singleness of purpose.

She had continued with her music mainly because her mother wanted her to. Gradually she had been realizing that her own desire was to be a dancer, but, not wanting to hurt her mother, she had smothered these emotions.

The conflict reached a peak when Betty Marie appeared in a piano and dance recital when she was twelve. In the first half of the recital she played the piano. The audience listened with respect and applauded with enthusiasm. Perhaps she should be a pianist, after all. It seemed right and good that she should, especially when she saw her mother's smiling face.

Then came the dance part. Floating about in a gossamer dress of soft yellow, Betty Marie knew that nothing could take the place of this. Dancing would be her world—a world she meant to conquer and her mother would have to understand.

The sisters were now to be taught by Madame Nijinska, the sister of the great Nijinsky, and also by David Lichine who had once danced with Pavlova. Both were strict disciplinarians, insisting on perfection and on complete mastery of every step. While Nijinska stressed preciseness, she also emphasized that it must be blended with emotion, that the dancer must be moved by and respond to the music. This Betty Marie understood, for her musical studies had developed her awareness of melody which would later find expression in her dancing.

Betty Marie was fifteen when she danced her first solo part in the Hollywood Bowl in a ballet based on a Chopin concerto, choreographed by Nijinska. Majorie also danced in this presentation. The ballet was well received and the critics praised the fledgling ballerina. Shortly after this, Betty Marie was offered the opportunity to study with the Ballet Russe in New York. But her mother refused to entertain any thought of a career until Betty Marie finished high school and hoped that she would attend the University of California.

To Betty Marie, however, dancing was as necessary as food and air and water. Not to dance was unthinkable. With her high school diploma in hand, she left for New York as soon as she could. But it was some time before she was accepted by a ballet company. Disappointed and discouraged, she thought she would have to return home when finally she was engaged by the Ballet Russe for a Canadian tour.

Before the company opened in Ottawa, there were hours and hours of fittings and rehearsals. Rest periods were brief, meals were snatched, and each day was exhausting. But to Betty Marie it was enchantment. She wrote home ecstatically—"All that matters is that I am dancing."

Because the road company was small, she had to learn more parts than would usually be the case, and with little time to do so. She never knew until almost the last moment what part she would dance, and sometimes the part would be changed when she was dressed and ready to go on stage.

But she stood out in every part that she danced in the corps de ballet, and gradually she was given small solos and minor roles that brought her to attention. When she danced the role of Spring in *Snow Maiden*, her dancing was praised as pure poetry and she was lavishly applauded. Newspaper critics predicted that she would become a great name in ballet.

All of this was music to her ears. She would have been very happy but for the animosity and jealousy of her fellow dancers. Because of Betty Marie's natural reserve and shyness, they thought her standoffish and reacted accordingly. Betty Marie very much wanted to be friendly, but her life had centered so much around her routine of practice and study and solitariness that she wasn't at ease with people.

The girls resented, also, that Betty Marie came from a moneyed family and was not so hard pressed financially as they. Most of all, they resented that she, a newcomer, was given featured parts and they were not.

So the backstage and offstage atmosphere was one of coldness, petty meanness, and barbed remarks. This all hurt so much that Betty Marie withdrew even more into herself and went about alone. It was like her school days when she had longed to go to parties and picnics and to have class chums, but never could. Only now, because she was away from home, she felt her lack of friends even more keenly. She grew pale and sad and suffered from Canada's cold weather.

After the Canadian tour, Betty Marie was signed on as a regular member of the Ballet Russe. She was told that she must work very hard and that she would receive important roles in time, but she would have to be patient for this would not be immediate. She was also told that she would meet with disappointment and frustration and constant pressure. If she could not stand up to the physical and mental demands that would be placed upon her, it would be best for her to leave.

Betty Marie signed the contract without hesitation. She was not afraid of any hardship, but would stay and become a top dancer, come what may. Dancing was all that mattered, all that would ever matter.

The director of the company suggested that she change her name to a Russian one. Most of those with Ballet Russe were Russian, and those who were not had assumed that identity. This Betty Marie stoutly refused to do. She agreed to change her first name to Maria, but her last name must remain as it was, she said. She did not object to it being spelled as one word, however, so that is what it became. The newspapers liked to refer to her as the beautiful dancing Osage princess, and they begged for stories about her life on the reservation when she "lived as an Indian." But Maria Tallchief had never done so and had no such stories to tell, and she would not permit the company's publicity department to glamorize her in this fashion. She would win her laurels on her ability as a dancer, and not on "being an Indian."

Six months after her arrival in New York City, Maria had a small part in *Rodeo*, a new ballet choreographed by Agnes de Mille. It was a tremendous success and did much to advance Maria's career. In spite of this, she was downcast and unhappy in spirit.

The Ballet Russe was to produce the Nijinska "E Minor Piano Concerto," usually called the "Chopin Concerto," in which Maria had first danced as a schoolgirl. The names of the cast had been posted but hers was not among them. She longed to do the concerto, for Nijinska had been a beloved teacher whom she had admired almost to idolatry. So well did she know the ballet that she could have filled in for any dancer. It was a blow to have to stand in the wings and watch others perform the familiar movements. She thought of the concerto as "her" ballet.

The ballet was a triumph and Maria rejoiced for her teacher and for those who had the star roles. At the same time, she grew increasingly depressed, for it seemed that all her efforts had gone unnoticed. No important roles had yet come her way.

She kept on, doggedly polishing and perfecting her dancing, however, practicing by herself and growing more wan, more thin, and more driven.

After a fall tour, when she danced in Los Angeles for the first time since leaving home, it seemed the chance she longed for had finally come. She was practicing by herself in preparation for the Christmas day opening when she was told that she should be ready to dance the concerto the following night. The ballerina in one of the starring roles was ill.

Her joy over this news was short-lived. As she waited in the wings ready to dance in this cherished role she was told that she would not be needed. The prima ballerina had decided that Maria had not had sufficient rehearsal time and could not master the difficult role in the short time given her.

This was such a crushing blow, that Maria ran from the theater to the solitude of her room. Never had her inner strength been put to greater test. Yet, in spite of her despair, she made herself return, head held high, to continue perfecting her technique.

She grew increasingly ill and barely got through the winter, dancing when she should not have done so, but unable to let down even for a moment. Her sister, Marjorie, had graduated from high school and was dancing with the Los Angeles Light Opera Company. It was a temptation to go home and find a place in the same company, as her mother begged her to do, but Maria stiffened her spine and hung on.

Then, on May 1, 1943, long awaited opportunity came. She was assigned to dance the concerto in the place of an ailing ballerina, a major soloist. It was the same role that Maria had first danced in the Hollywood Bowl.

Her performance in the Concerto was so sparkling, so radiant, it was recognized at once that here was a dancer of magnitude who would undoubtedly become a prima ballerina—who was not far from that exalted status even then. The applause was deafening, and the older ballerinas stood aside and applauded also.

From then on, Maria danced the concerto whenever it was presented. She danced the ballet's debut in New York City when she was eighteen years old to a tremendous ovation. Bouquets of flowers were heaped on the stage, among them an armful of American Beauty roses from the corps girls who had tormented her so in the past.

The young girl whose only desire was to be a dancer had became a celebrity. When the concerto was announced, people flocked to see her more than they did to see the ballet. She was the object of adulation that could easily have turned the head of one so young. But surprisingly, she was not given other important roles, or roles that were suited to her. Again she grew discouraged.

When George Balanchine took over the direction of the company, he selected Maria for the understudy role in *The Song of Norway*. Balanchine had created some of the brightest of the ballet stars. He saw in Maria one whom he could shape into the brightest of all. She had the dedication and the inner spark that waited only a touch of magic.

Maria was very happy dancing for Balanchine. She had always formed an attachment for her teachers, and she looked up to Balanchine as "the most marvelous of men." She worked for him tirelessly, doing over and over what he asked or wanted, exactly as he said, and taking on more and more depth as a dancer.

Marjorie was now in New York, too. She had been chosen by the great ballerina, Alicia Markova, and personally coached for the part of Myrtha in the ballet *Giselle*. Her success in this role led to her appointment as a soloist with the American Ballet Theatre. The two sisters dazzled New York audiences, and it became the fashion to go from one theater to the other at the times when both were performing. Yet, as fond as they were of each other, neither sister ever saw the other one dance.

Under Balanchine, Maria became sensational. He knew exactly how to cast her, how to display her fluid grace and amazing skill. Her performances were described as sheer magic. No matter how difficult the role, and they grew increasingly difficult, if Balanchine said she could do it, Maria did.

Her audiences would hardly let her leave the stage, screaming their pleasure and demanding more and still more. Although the critics had long before given her the title of ballerina, Ballet Russe, surprisingly, had not. She was still listed as a soloist. A dancer had to prove herself many times before the status of ballerina was conferred in this company, which adhered so closely to the Russian tradition.

Although Balanchine was twenty years older than Maria, they had strong ties aside from that of master and student. A love of music, for one thing, brought them together, and nobody was surprised when their marriage was announced.

Balanchine resigned from Ballet Russe, but Maria remained to complete her contract. Now that she was a star of first rank, Ballet Russe decided that she had really earned the ballerina title—the first American in the history of the company to hold it. She was urged to remain with the company, but she preferred to go with her husband to Paris.

In her final weeks with the Ballet Russe she colored every role she danced with her own personality. She had almost completely changed from the shy, withdrawn young girl that she had been. She was vivid, vibrant, alight with happiness and success. Wherever she went she was mobbed by fans and people waited in line for hours to see her. Her performances were sellouts. Nobody thought that she would cast all of this aside and leave, but Maria had no other desire than to be with Balanchine.

Marjorie had already gone to France. She was dancing with the Grand Ballet of the Marquis de Cuevas in Monte Carlo where she was to become a ballerina when she was nineteen.

In Paris, Balanchine presented Maria in one of her greatest roles, *The Fairy's Kiss.* No American had danced at the Paris Opera in more than one hundred years and Parisians were angered by what they considered "effrontery." They came to "boo" and they went away stunned by what they had seen. They talked of little else and clamored to see the "extraordinary Indian."

It was perhaps the electric response to Maria, combined with her own outstanding ability, that opened the way more quickly for Marjorie as the first American to become Priemière Danseuse Étoile of the Paris Opera. She was also the first American to dance with the Paris Opera Ballet at the Bolshoi Theatre in Moscow.

Marjorie had made her permanent home in France. She married her dance partner, George Skibine, and rose to her own heights, dancing many of the same roles that her sister did, but always in her own inimitable way.

She danced before President John F. Kennedy and President Charles de Gaulle during President Kennedy's visit to France, and she appeared before a number of European crowned heads. She was honored by the Tunisian government for her artistic achievements.

Back in New York, new triumphs awaited Maria. But for a time, her career suffered. Audiences wanted to see her in new dramatic roles, but she could dance only what was created for her. Balanchine, however, was not producing. As so often happens with highly talented people, he had come to a stalemate in his creative expression. People openly wondered if he and Maria could overcome this fallow period.

In 1949, Balanchine at last choreographed the ballet that was to be the peak in Maria's career. This was his version of *The Firebird*. Maria had only one week to learn the part, and Balanchine drove her as she had never been driven before. She was no longer to be "Balanchine's Ballerina,"—she was to be Maria Tallchief, the queen of ballet, standing alone, supreme, soaring to a place where no one could follow.

Few believed that she could excel in this Russian ballet which demanded the utmost in emotional shadings. Maria was regal, splendid, the glamorous but aloof Snow Princess in a crystal palace. It was she who would carry the full responsibility for the success of the ballet. Balanchine's name—and hers—were at stake.

Maria danced as though enchanted. In awesome control, she *was* the firebird, a mystic creature enveloped in a sheath of flame. She was so exciting that the audience sat spellbound in silence for a moment before their ecstatic applause cannonaded through the theater. In that one performance, Maria Tallchief was transformed into a prima ballerina. From then on, only the choicest roles would be hers.

It was not long after this triumph that Maria was shattered by the breakup of her marriage. Balanchine had helped her develop her artistry to an unsurpassing

brilliance. Now he felt Maria must be free of every bind-
ing, dependent relationship, free to use that artistry to
its fullest—and he must be free to find a new dancer.

It was very difficult, at first, for Maria to understand
and accept this, or to see that Balanchine, by his very
nature, could act no differently. She brooded for some
time, but then the hurt began to ease and the discipline
of the years asserted itself. Once again she was the great
artist and even greater dancer.

A European tour took her to a number of countries
and in each, the critics said that they had "seen the performance of a lifetime." The tour was the needed ther-
apy. Her spirits revived and Maria was once more in
love. She married a young charter airline pilot.

For the next two years, she traveled constantly and
was hailed the world over. What she danced made no
difference. People just wanted to see her and there was
an outpouring of tributes from every corner of the
globe.

The Osages, too, honored her with a special name-
giving ceremony and the title of Princess. Her name
(Wa-Xthe-Thonbe) was chosen by her grandmother and
meant Woman of Two Standards. It expressed the
thought that Maria belonged to two worlds, the Osage
world and the world at large. She had upheld the dignity of the Osages while winning acclaim from others.

No ovation was ever to be so meaningful as this recognition from her own people.

Her husband began to tire of marriage to an international star and pressed her to give up dancing. This she
could not do. She had contractual commitments and a
personal dedication to her profession. As she had chosen
dancing over music, she chose it again over marriage.

Although she grieved over this new sorrow and felt
emotionally drained and empty, she was not quite as
devastated as she had been over Balanchine. She was

now a person of greater maturity and a much finer dancer. There was no role that she could not dance with sensitivity and with an indelible imprint that was entirely hers. She was a living legend—in South America, in Canada, in the Orient, in the Middle East, in Europe—the reigning queen of ballet with throngs of admiring subjects wherever she performed.

Now, with the world at her feet, she began to think of having a home and a family. Marjorie, dividing her time between France and her old home in Oklahoma, had two handsome sons and was still winning new laurels as a dancer.

Once more Maria fell in love, this time with a Chicago businessman named Henry D. Paschen, Jr. Although he had little understanding of ballet, he understood Maria and accepted her desire to continue dancing. He gave her every support.

They were married in 1956 and for a while Maria continued to draw record audiences to her scintillating performances. Inwardly, however she had begun to look forward to retirement. Shortly after the birth of her daughter, Lisa, she put her ballet shoes away forever without regret or any feeling of conflict. One life was over and a new one had begun. Happiness lay with her husband, her daughter, and her home.

Maria Tallchief lives in Chicago where she is an active participant in civic and social affairs and is even now the recipient of varied honors. In 1967 she received the Indian Achievement Award and most recently was elected to the Oklahoma Hall of Fame and was honored by Rockford College with the Jane Addams Award.

In 1965, Marjorie created the title role of Ariadne for the Harkness Ballet and later appeared in a new ballet, *The Four Moons* based on an Indian theme and written by Louis Ballard, a Cherokee-Quapaw Indian. The ballet was presented in Oklahoma in connection with ceremonies related to the sixtieth anniversary of statehood. Appearing with her were three other Oklahoma-born ballerinas of Indian blood—Roselle Hightower (Choctaw), Yvonne Choteau (Cherokee) and Moscelyne Larkin (Shawnee).

WILMA L. VICTOR

EDUCATOR IN
GOVERNMENT

Wilma Victor has spent her entire life in the educational field in service to Indian youth. At present, as special assistant to Secretary of the Interior Morton, she holds a very important government post, the highest to be held by an Indian woman.

Wilma was born in Idabel, Oklahoma. Her parents, both fullblood Choctaws, had sold their holdings in the country and moved to town so that their children could have the advantages of public schooling.

The Choctaw tribe was the largest of those tribes that originally lived in Mississippi and Alabama. They were first in contact with the whites when De Soto attacked their town of Maubila in 1540. Tuskalusa, the chief, and his warriors fought bravely but the town was destroyed and burned to the ground.

The Choctaws were farmers and excelled in growing corn. They were a peace-loving people, but they were great fighters if forced to defend themselves. To protect their villages from invasion, they built towns on their eastern border called barrier towns. These were for the purpose of front-line defense.

When the French came into the area, they formed a strong friendship with the Choctaw and were politically aligned with them for many years. Later, the Choctaws came under the influence of the Spaniards and remained so until after the War of 1812.

In 1803, when the United States completed the Louisiana Purchase, the Choctaws were acknowledged as the owners of more than 14 million acres of land. The tribe was friendly to the new government and more than once helped it to subdue other tribes bent on causing trouble. In 1805, they ceded a large tract of land for white settlement, and for some time they lived peacefully with the settlers. During those years the Choctaws instituted many social reforms. They abolished the practice of witchcraft, established schools, and improved their standards of living.

In the War of 1812, the Choctaws, as guides and warriors, fought with Andrew Jackson and helped in the defeat of the British in the seige of New Orleans. They felt that this entitled them to keep their ancestral lands, but by 1820, they were forced to cede 5½ million acres in Mississippi in exchange for land in Indian Territory. They still held on to a million acres in the forlorn hope that they would not have to yield to the mounting pressure for their removal to the west.

In the meantime, thousands of settlers swarmed into the ceded territory and by 1830 there was no longer any hope that the Choctaws could stay. In the Treaty of Dancing Rabbit Creek, all of their land was taken, and by 1838, the Choctaws had made the tragic march over the Trail of Tears.

The southern part of Indian Territory was assigned to the Choctaws. The sufferings of the people on the march to the west were as dreadful as they were in attempting to get reestablished in Oklahoma. The forebears of Wilma's parents came over the trail and lost many of their relatives. Others were lost in Indian Territory when there was a tuberculosis epidemic.

Those who survived the march and the epidemic gradually recovered from the ordeal, reconstructed their government, and opened several schools called seminaries. Both of Wilma's parents attended these early seminaries, and had impressed upon them the tribe's dedication to education.

Indian Territory and Oklahoma Territory were merged when Oklahoma was admitted to the union as the forty-sixth state. The Choctaws, along with the other groups known as the Five Civilized Tribes that had come from the east, united with non-Indians under one form of government. The name *Oklahoma* is a Choctaw word meaning "red people."

The Victors lived in the area known as the Old Choctaw Nation, the heart of the former Choctaw territory. Many of the people who had knowledge of early Choctaw customs and history lived there, and Wilma, as a girl, saw them and listened to their stories. They too stressed that it was important for their young people to go to school and to be educated.

So Wilma, her sister, and her two brothers, all went to the town schools and looked forward to going to college.

By the time Wilma completed high school, however, a college education seemed out of the question. College tuition was expensive and the financing would be a problem. However, her friend, Taphia Slater, a Choctaw who was a social worker with the Bureau of Indian Affairs, saw in Wilma someone with a great deal of promise and secured for her a working scholarship to the University of Kansas. Wilma could live at Haskell Indian School while she was attending the university. This program had been worked out by the Bureau of Indian Affairs at a time of expanding Indian education and for Wilma it was a wonderful opportunity.

There were so many poor families around her home, that she thought she would go into social work, too, and her mind was set on this goal. She was delighted to be at Haskell, where she met Indians from all parts of the country. While she lived in Oklahoma, she knew only her own tribal group and was scarcely aware that there were others.

Toward the end of Wilma's two-year course at the University of Kansas, she was approached by the Director of Education for the Bureau of Indian Affairs, Dr. Willard Beatty. There was a great lack of Indian teachers and they were needed badly. If Wilma would agree to continue her education and become a teacher, a larger scholarship could be provided for her.

During her years in school, Wilma had broadened her horizons considerably. She wanted something challenging and she remembered now the emphasis placed on education by her Choctaw people. To be educated is to meet the white man on his own terms, they said. To be educated is to be able to receive and absorb all that the white man has to offer and to weave it into opportunity for ourselves. Without the education of the white man, Indians will never be able to think and act for themselves, but will always be dependent upon the white man.

Her resolve to go into teaching was further strengthed by Ruth Muskrat Bronson, a Cherokee, who was guidance and scholarship officer for the Bureau of Indian Affairs. She came often to Haskell and Wilma talked with her.

Ruth Bronson came from hill country in Oklahoma. She was well aware that not all Oklahoma Indians were oil-rich and that many had serious problems fitting into a modern life that seemed to have no room for their ideals or backgrounds.

Like Wilma, she had attended public school and the University of Kansas. She was later graduated from Mt. Holyoke College and did graduate work at George Washington University. In 1922, she represented Indian students at a world conference in Peking, China. She was the first teacher of English at Haskell before becoming a guidance and placement officer.

Ruth Bronson, too, pointed out the great need for a better trained Indian leadership. And Wilma, with the deep sense of responsibility for her race, common to many Indian young people, was won over to teaching.

The University of Kansas did not, at that time, have a strong program in teacher training, so Wilma was enrolled at the Milwaukee State Teachers College, now the University of Wisconsin (Milwaukee). It was there she obtained her bachelor's degree to which she would later add her master's in education from the University of Oklahoma.

Her first assignment was an apprentice teacher on the Navajo reservation at Shiprock, New Mexico. This was an introduction to old Indian culture, for the Navajos had retained many of their traditional ways. Most of the parents did not wish to send their children to school even if there were schools to accept them.

At that time the majority of Navajo children did not attend school, some because there was no school nearby, others because their parents would not let them attend. The children at Shiprock were in school because they wanted to be there. They were eager to learn and this desire on the part of their pupils was a delight to the teachers.

The school was much more than a school—it was a community center. Navajo mothers brought their washing to the school and old men came and sat around and talked. At Shiprock, Wilma came to know and understand many of the Navajo people.

When World War II broke out, Wilma considered the idea of enlisting. One day, she went into Santa Fe and entered the post office to buy some stamps. A WAC recruiter was there. Wilma came out with her stamps, but also as an enlisted member of the Women's Army Corps.

She was given her basic training in Florida. Then she was sent to various camps over the country. Her officer's training was completed at Fort Des Moines, Iowa. She was in military intelligence for a while. Then she was sent to Fort Campbell, Kentucky, where her duties were executive and administrative and where she was finally mustered out after the war ended.

She returned to Oklahoma and taught in the public schools for a while. Then she was asked to return to the Bureau of Indian Affairs as a teacher. A new, large school had been established in Utah to teach Navajo students who were now clamoring for an education. They came to the Intermountain School with little or no schooling and many could speak no English.

Wilma helped to develop three educational programs for these youngsters. She is most proud of the eight-year program. The youngsters who entered this program could stay at the school long enough to receive full preparation to enter high school directly from Intermountain. Many of them did go on to high school, even if they were over age.

After thirteen years, with the Navajo program underway and going well, she was sent to Santa Fe to assist in the opening of the Institute of American Indian Arts. This unique institution, in addition to its academic program, concentrates on all phases of the arts that are either native Indian in origin, such as weaving and pottery, or adaptive to Indian application, such as traditional legends adapted for the modern stage. Wilma developed the academic curriculum in connection with this institution.

Then she was asked to return to Intermountain as supervisor. While there, she was selected to receive, with five other women, the Federal Women's Award for 1967. The winners represent highest achievement in the fields of chemistry, diplomacy, education, housing, medicine, and pathology. She was the only Indian to receive this award, and her citation read that it was given because "under her direction, thousands of Navajo adolescents of widely varying ability and background were provided with personal, social, academic, and educational skills to fit them for employment, broaden their opportunities, and lift their aspirations." Her brilliant, innovative leadership in keeping pace with constantly changing situations and maintaining harmonious relationships between school and community; her personal enthusiasm; her wide range of interest; and her high professional standards were also cited as an inspiration to her associates.

Wilma's exceptional creative and executive ability in the administration of a unique and complex school program for disadvantaged Indian young people had made her the top woman educator in the Indian Service, and a top personality in the entire educational field. She was asked to speak at educational conferences, was the keynote speaker for the first National Indian Workshop for Indian Affairs, and addressed the National Education Association at the twentieth anniversary of the White House Council on Rural Education. The state of Utah named her as one of "seven women of the '70s."

In 1971, Wilma Victor was named special assistant to Secretary of the Interior Rogers C. B. Morton, a newly created post that has placed her among the most important women in government circles. In the post she acts as liaison between agencies and foundations that work with Indian people and programs. She shuns the word "problems," but agrees that Indian difficulties have to be solved by Indian self-determination. The tribes will have to make their own decisions, she says, for this is "the only realistic and practical way to expedite the procedures needed to make us stand up as true citizens. The diversity of Indian laws and lifestyles underscores the need for consultation with Indians themselves. We are perfectly capable of charting our own course."

A year before this appointment, Ms. Victor received the Indian Achievement Award, which was presented to her before the Sequoya statue in the Capitol. Sequoya was the Cherokee genius who developed an alphabet for his people, thereby giving them the advantage of a written language. He is called the Indian Cadmus.

Ms. Victor's years of service to Indian youth has made her keenly aware of the challenges and opportunities facing them. "If I am hung up on anything," she says with a smile, "it is that Indian young people must be brought into educational planning, earlier and earlier and with all kinds of adults. They must be brought into discussions and into decision making. They are able to talk and express their views, and our big mistake is in telling them what's good for them. They can make changes in the educational plan that will be for the overall good and they should be allowed to do it."

ELAINE ABRAHAM RAMOS

COLLEGE VICE-PRESIDENT

Diminutive dynamo is a description that could well be applied to Elaine Ramos of the Tlingits. This tiny, energetic woman has a tremendous capacity for involvement and constantly demonstrates an active concern for others. Her name in Tlingit, Lax ya Koosè ix, means everlasting, and undoubtedly the results of her accomplishments will live far beyond her span on earth.

The Tlingits, a northwest coast tribe, shared in the wonderfully unique culture of the area. They were sea rovers who roamed the coast in their huge canoes fashioned from giant cedar trees, hunting the ocean for food and living entirely from the catch. They were master carvers and builders, and their totem poles were among the finest. Their rituals and ceremonies were in the form of dramatic plays and pageants given by elaborately masked and costumed dancers and chanters.

The history of the Tlingits goes back thousands of years, and out of their past they preserved an oral record of their legends, myths, and traditions. They were in contact with European fur traders in search of the valuable sea otter as early as 1786. By 1788, the Russians arrived and there was continual conflict, for the Indians were cruelly exploited. In 1836, half of the tribe died from smallpox, and gradually they were overcome by the Russian occupation.

The United States bought Alaska from Russia in 1867, and again newcomers were drawn by the riches of the natural resources, much to the detriment of the natives. On their heels came missionaries and gold seekers and the Tlingit culture deteriorated further. Eventually, their rituals and language were outlawed, and they gradually adopted white customs.

Elaine's father, Olaf Abraham, came from a family of nobles. Unlike tribes in other parts of the country, the Tlingits, and other northwest Indians had a distinct status system of nobles and commoners. Olaf Abraham was one of the first Christian converts among the Tlingits, but he always adhered to the cultural and social traditions of his people. He was over a hundred when he died and the last forty years of his life were spent in the service of the Presbyterian Church.

"His hand and his footprint were in every phase of history of the Yakutat area," his daughter says. "He had a hand in building the first cannery, the railroad, the hospital, and the school. He greeted everyone with understanding, compassion, and love. From him came my own strength, determination, and love for all men."

Elaine was born in the tiny, isolated village of Yakutat which lies in the most northern part of Tlingit country. The youngest of four children, she grew up in a bilingual home. In the evening, her father told of Tlingit history and traditions, speaking only in the Tlingit language. Her mother spoke both Tlingit and English, reading from the Bible and from what few books were available in the village day school.

"I have never ceased to be thankful that my parents

brought us up in this way," Elaine says. "My knowledge of Tlingit culture has enriched my whole life. Now that only a thread of our culture and language exists, I have something from the past of great meaning."

Olaf was a commercial fisherman, and in the summer the family lived in a fishing camp. In the fall they moved to another fishing camp where they dried fish and picked berries and dried them for winter use. In the spring, the family lived in a seal camp. They dried seal meat, rendered the fat for oil, and tanned the hides for moccasins. From the middle of October until April, Elaine went to school.

When she was old enough, she was sent to a federal boarding school and completed her high school studies in a private school in Sitka.

When she decided that she would like to become a nurse, she was helped to obtain a scholarship at Sage Memorial Hospital in Arizona. She was the first Tlingit to enter the nursing profession.

Her father's mother was a nurse in the Indian way, treating those who were ill with herbs. She could also do suturing, using the gut from porpoises for her suturing material. She thinks that the stories she heard about this grandmother planted the seeds that motivated her to nursing.

After Elaine graduated, she answered a call for nurses on the Navajo reservation. According to Navajo history, the tribe had a northern origin, which seems to be confirmed by the similarity in Navajo and Tlingit words. Elaine got along with the people and had no difficulties of a language barrier.

The Navajos at that time did not readily accept the white man or his medicine, and they were very superstitious about death. Providing them with medical care was very frustrating and nurses did not stay long, for they became discouraged by the frustrations and the remote country.

The experience, however, was valuable to Elaine and would be put to good use in the years ahead. The isolation did not bother her, for she had grown up in isolation. She delivered babies on her hands and knees in Navajo hogans, and nursed many patients through a frightening diptheria epidemic.

Returning to Yakutat, she carried on with her nursing under the most primitive conditions. She was the only person in the village with any knowledge of medicine. The nearest hospital was at Juneau, three hundred miles away. Some of her experiences were examples of sheer heroism.

She recalls that once, during a severe rain storm, she had two patients in labor. They lived a mile from each other, and both had serious birth problems. All through the night Elaine sloshed back and forth in the heavy downpour from one patient to the other. She finally made it to the cannery building and was able to send out a radio call for help. An oil company sent a plane and picked up the patients and took them to Juneau. While Elaine doesn't say it, it is easy to tell that this was a life-saving mission.

At another time, she saved the life of a six-year-old boy who was dying of pneumonia. When Elaine was called, the boy was turning blue from lack of oxygen. Sending out an SOS, Elaine pleaded for any plane to answer the call for help. A blinding snowstorm was raging, but an Air Force plane landed and picked up the child for transfer to an Air Force hospital at Anchorage. Elaine went along to care for the boy and administer oxygen.

At the time this happened, she was very much involved in a struggle over discrimination between the school for whites and the school for Natives at Yakutat. (The term Native is used in Alaska to distinguish the Indians, Eskimos, and Aleuts whose forebears were the original inhabitants from the white newcomers.) The father of the boy whose life she saved was president of the school board and the fight was a bitter one. Feelings were hardly friendly but this in no way affected her dedication to duty.

The schools at Yakutat are now coordinated and all Native schools receive state educational services.

When there was a diptheria epidemic in the Eskimo country, Elaine volunteered for nursing duty, working in many remote parts of Alaska where there were no doctors.

This caused her to turn her attention to finding a way to establish a health aid program for the isolated Native villages. With the help of a medical friend, she initiated the Southeast Health Aid Program, which trained the village people in simple procedures and provided medical instruction in emergencies through a radio hookup. At first, there was much opposition to such a plan, but Elaine continued to press for it and was finally able to get it started in one village. A village was added each year for seven years. The program, with expanded teaching, is now state wide. Later, she helped to initiate the Alaska Board of Health, which provided opportunity to the people to have some control over health care programs and to actively participate in them. This is now called the Alaska Native Health Board, and it too is a state-wide operation.

These genuinely innovative programs are administered by the Public Health Service. They include the Native people as partners in planning and starting health projects and training, giving them the chance to enter and advance in the health professions.

Twenty years ago, Elaine says, there was not an Indian or Eskimo family in all Alaska that was not touched by tuberculosis, especially tuberculosis of the bones. Now this illness is of only minor incidence. Today, the greatest problem is alcoholism. She attributes this, at least partly to the breakup of families caused by the removal of those afflicted with tuberculosis to hospitals. The family ties among Indians are very strong, she says, and the separations removed the family control and broke down the family unity.

Another reason for the increase in alcoholism she believes to be the influx of soldiers during World War II, when bases were established near Yakutat. The village, which had been entirely isolated, suffered under the contact with the "outside."

Elaine Ramos spent a year from 1965 to 1966 in Cleveland, Ohio, as a floor nurse for a large hospital, then she returned to Alaska to serve as surgical supervising nurse at the Mt. Edgecumbe Medical Unit. She advanced to the position of night supervisor, completely in charge of all of the hospital and personnel. She resigned this position to continue her education at Sheldon Jackson College and graduated as salutatorian of her class.

She became assistant dean of students at this college and in 1972 was appointed vice-president.

Sheldon Jackson College, the oldest school in Alaska in continuous operation, was first opened by Presbyterian missionaries. It is a fully-accredited two-year junior college, especially oriented to the training of Native students in the arts and sciences. Elaine Ramos's position is a liaison one. She participates in many educational conferences and travels a great deal as representative of the college in various activities.

One of her major personal activities has been a group called the Raven Dancers. About twenty years ago, her father began to revive the old culture among the Tlingits. He said that he had watched white education for eighty years, and Indians, since giving up their own, were "dying." To regain their original strength, they needed to bring back the old ways. So, although he was then in his seventies, he began to teach the old songs and dances to those who cared about them.

It was natural for Elaine to become interested. With her husband, George, whom she married in the mid-fifties and their children Charmaine, Judith, George Jr., and David, she founded the Raven Dancers about eight years ago. The group has appeared all over Alaska and also in the "lower states." This is an Indian presentation that is entirely different from the usual singing and dancing that has become fairly commonplace to American audiences. The costuming, alone, is fantastic, and a relatively unknown side of Indian life is portrayed authentically.

Another project is the development of a Tlingit and Haida Language Workshop to assist the Native people in the restoration of their languages at a vital part of their heritage. Elaine Ramos coordinated and directed this project. She is looked up to by her people as a professional nurse and as a dedicated educator.

BIBLIOGRAPHY

Abeita, Louise. *I Am a Pueblo Indian Girl*. New York: William Morrow & Co., 1939.

Bennett, Kay. *Kai-bah*. Los Angeles: Westernlore Press, 1964.

Bronson, Ruth Muskrat. *Indians Are People, Too*. New York: Friendship Press, 1942.

Crary, Margaret. *Susette La Flesche—Voice of the Omaha Indians*. New York: Hawthorn Books, 1973.

Crowell, Ann. *A Hogan for the Bluebird*. New York: Charles Scribner's Sons, 1969.

deLeeuw, Adele. *Maria Tallchief, American Ballerina*. Champaign: Garrard Publishing Co., 1971.

Deloria, Ella C. *Speaking of Indians*. New York: Friendship Press, 1942.

Farnsworth, Frances, J. *Winged Moccasins: The Story of Sacajawea*. New York: Julian Messner, 1954.

Frazier, Neta L. *Sacajawea, the Girl Nobody Knows*. New York: David McKay, 1967.

Henderstadt, Dorothy. *Marie Tanglehair*. New York: David McKay, 1965.

Hopkins, Sarah Winnemucca. *Life Among the Paiutes*. New York: G. P. Putnam's Sons, 1883.

Howard, Harold P. *Sacajawea*. Norman: University of Oklahoma Press, 1971.

Jones, David E. *Sanapin: Comanche Medicine Woman*. New York: Holt, Rinehart & Winston, 1972.

Johnson, E. Pauline. *Flint and Feather*. New York: G. P. Putnam's Sons, 1883.

Lowry, Annie. *Karnee: A Paiute Narrative.* Las Vegas: University of Nevada Press, 1966.

Marriot, Alice. *Maria, the Potter of San Ildefonso.* Norman: University of Oklahoma Press, 1948.

Maynard, Olga. *Bird of Fire.* New York: Dodd, Mead & Co., 1961.

Myers, Elizabeth. *Maria Tallchief.* New York: Grosset & Dunlap, 1967.

Nelson, Mary Carroll. *Annie Wauneka.* North Minneapolis: Dillon Press, 1972.

Nelson, Mary Carroll. *Maria Martinez.* North Minneapolis: Dillon Press, 1972.

Nelson, Mary Carroll. *Pablita Velarde.* North Minneapolis: Dillon Press, 1971.

O'Dell, Scott. *Island of the Blue Dolphins.* Boston: Houghton Mifflin Co., 1960.

O'Meara, Walter. *Daughters of the Country.* New York: Harcourt Brace Jovanovich, 1968.

Penny, Grace Jackson. *Moki.* Boston: Houghton Mifflin Co., 1960.

Quyawayma, Polingayai. *No Turning Back.* Albuquerque: University of New Mexico Press, 1964.

Seibert, Jerry. *Sacajawea: Guide to Lewis and Clarke.* Boston: Houghton Mifflin Co., 1960.

Sekaquaptewa, Helen. *Me and Mine.* Tucson: University of Arizona Press, 1969.

Velarde, Pablita. *Old Father, the Story Teller.* New York: Globe Book Co., 1960.

Voss, Caroll. *White Cap for Rechinda.* New York: Ives Washburn, 1966.

Wahl, Jan. *Pocahontas in London.* New York: Delacorte Press, 1967.

Waltrip, Lela and Rufus. *Indian Women.* New York: David McKay, 1964.

Wilkie, Katherine E. *Pocahontas, Indian Princess.* Champaign: Garrard Publishing Co., 1969.

Winnie, Lucille. *Sah-Gan-De-Oh.* New York: Vantage Press, 1969.

Woodward, Grace Steele. *Pocahontas.* Norman: University of Oklahoma Press, 1969.

Wyess, Thelma Hatch. *Star Girl.* New York: Viking Press, 1967.

INDEX